GREEN

2

GOLDEN

CUSTOMER SUCCESS THAT PRODUCES REAL ROI

JACKIE GOLDEN

PUBLISHED BY

 LandNExpand

GREEN 2 GOLDEN
CUSTOMER SUCCESS THAT PRODUCES REAL ROI
BY JACKIE GOLDEN

Published by:
Published by LandNExpand, LLC

Book Cover, Interior Layout and Design | Yvonne Parks | PearCreative.ca

Printed in the USA

Print ISBN: 978-0-9967831-2-5
Ebook ISBN:978-0-9967831-4-9

DEDICATION

This book is dedicated to my loving husband, Jerry Golden, who has been my best friend, supporter of my career and mentor for the last 38 years. I would not be who I am today without him as my life long partner.

TABLE OF CONTENTS

FOREWORD

I grew up as the son of a software entrepreneur.

My father would share with me wisdom from his experience in the working world. One of his favorite things to say was "Son, in business you're either building the product or selling it." But after spending the last 17 years building technology companies of my own, I now understand that today's economy is radically different from the one in which my father operated.

You see, today, your success as a business is inextricably linked to the success of your customers. This goes far beyond building and selling product -- if your customers aren't realizing radical value from your products or services, renewing their contracts, referring you to other customers, etc., your bottom line as a company is at risk.

We spend a lot of time at Gainsight helping evangelize this message to the world. We call this new mindset of orienting around the customer, Customer Success. This isn't just a clever buzzword tied to rhetoric, but a full-fledged business practice that the leading companies in the world are employing to drive revenue.

One of the key tenants of Customer Success is to align all customer touch points around a well-executed customer experience model as a means of growing your installed base of loyal customers. Although great "customer service" has been a hot discussion topic over the last 10 years, the idea of building the ultimate customer experience goes further to involve every functional area of the company.

Jackie's approach to building a Customer Life Cycle model as the heart of a company's customer experience framework is powerful for companies to build customers for life with consistency and quality. It will give your company a competitive edge and the ability to drive innovation and thought leadership capabilities within your teams. Her passion for creating the kind of success for customers that is truly indispensable to how the company operates is infectious. She challenges you to really understand the customer's perception of how effective your product is in providing improved operational effectiveness, innovation capabilities or driving revenue and growth. My favorite quote is *"The customer's perception is my reality."*

I have read many great business books over the years and what I love about this book is that it is an excellent implementation guide for building the foundational elements that create a strong basis for the organizations to work together better with the customer experience as the focus. Jackie shares her secrets for how she has helped some of the top software companies find tremendous success and high growth profitably by using this customer experience framework as the center of her strategy.

I believe that if more companies embrace this approach to their go-to market strategies, they would find this to be a shorter pathway to attaining healthy (and sustainable) growth. The rich content Jackie shares with a logical and easy to follow implementation methodology will provide many organizations a great way to build their customer experience models that will work.

As more businesses are embracing a subscription-based pricing model, investing in Customer Success (early) is no longer an optional exercise. Your customers are your company's growth engine. With the principles Jackie describes in *Green 2 Golden*, you've now got the definitive playbook for delivering an end-to-end customer experience focused on driving unparalleled degrees of success for your customers, and therefore, to your company.

I'll be sure to send my father a copy.

Nick Mehta, CEO
Gainsight

INTRODUCTION

"Customer experience," or CX, has become a hot topic in the past decade. This guide will show you how to build a world-class customer experience model that delivers a results-driven approach that ensures a consistent, repeatable, and quality customer experience for your clients over the long term.

As an executive with 30 years' corporate experience and 20 years in high tech, I have helped dozens of companies develop a successful customer experience model. This book builds on those results to share proven strategies that work. This model has been developed over the last 20 years from my experience building a customer experience approach in the high tech industry for companies like Hyperion, Cognos, Ascential, IBM, and Workfront (formerly AtTask). I have optimized the model over time by targeting what works in order to build the best results-driven customer experience model.

In short, the most successful customer experience model generates an increase in sales and long-term customer fans in a profitable way. The model I have found successful and executed at many successful software companies created a consistent approach to selling and servicing customers that increased sales, created a profitable services organization, ensured high renewal rates, and provided an increase in customer expansion growth rates. The secret was in finding the real value for each customer. I have continued to work with high growth, high tech companies to help them build a customer experience model with the right strategies using precise execution plans, built on proven models that provides their customers with the right customer experience to hook them and provide on-going value and return on their investment (ROI).

CHAPTER 1

THE BENEFITS OF A CUSTOMER FOCUSED BUSINESS MODEL AND STRATEGY

Over the last 20 years, I have had the pleasure of working with hundreds of customers, specifically in the high tech industry, helping them implement software solutions that were designed to revolutionize their business and to provide a competitive edge.

As many of you have probably experienced, thoughtful and strategic use of technology provides a significant edge to innovation capabilities, operational effectiveness, automation, employee capacity and productivity, and many more operational improvements.

Many great technology companies have helped transform top corporations worldwide with their hardware, software and various product innovations. Most of these innovations have focused on improving specific aspects of a corporation. For example, financial reporting with improved transparencies and insights. In addition, there was the business intelligence craze, which offered dashboard reporting on key Performance Indicators (KPIs).

Then we had the ERP revelation in automating manufacturing and tracking more insightful information to find ways to reduce costs. Remember, too, the Master Data Management era that uncovered the power of quality data versus bad data and how to maintain "one source of the truth". Of course, my favorite is the latest around Big Data Analytics and the ability for technology to actually learn from the data and provide answers and predictions.

Wait! What happened to the customer experience? Notice that in all these innovations to help companies succeed and grow, the focus was never really about what the customer was experiencing as part of the strategic formula for success. It was a combination of management techniques, with a solid strategic plan, that created the right corporate climate, which followed a concise dashboard of key metrics and targets, with the right people on the bus who were motivated in the right ways, creating an excellent quality product. Finally, there was the idea of a solid customer support team. However, a customer success program or the development of all of the above elements lacked a focus on the customer's expectations and the value required to be a transformative solution for the customer. The perspective of the corporate strategy was based on what a company thought the customer wanted. Most corporations start with what is our target customer market, what problems are we solving and what is our solution to solving those problems. While this will help drive a solid go to market strategy, it is missing one of the key aspects to driving long term performance; the customer's perception and expectations and ultimately an ROI worth their continuous investment.

Only in the last five to ten years has the concept of creating a customer success plan become critical in creating a successful company.

MAKING A DIFFERENCE AT HYPERION FOCUSED ON THE CUSTOMER

When I left the corporate finance world and joined my first technology company, Hyperion, as a consultant, my focus right from the beginning was listening to what the customer was trying to accomplish and finding the best solution for them using the Hyperion products.

Ultimately I created my own methodology, which became my personal approach to consulting with each customer to whom I was assigned. In fact, Hyperion created a methodology shortly after I joined. And I was able to contribute to the final outcome. However, I was determined to influence our focus around creating a better solution for the customer. I felt that we should focus on what would make the most impactful financial solution for each customer based on the best practices for their industry and not just the basic financial reporting requirements.

The Hyperion methodology team was focused on creating a best practice approach with a prescriptive step by step set of tasks that all consultants should follow and documents that were required to be delivered on each assignment. As Hyperion evolved into a larger company with multiple products, the methodology began to falter because we didn't have a best practice approach to designing a robust, impactful end-to-end solution using all of our products so that the customer would receive a clear vision of the final solution with a detailed roadmap of how to get from where they were to the ultimate vision.

Don't get me wrong, I have also worked with customers that had no idea where to start or even what they wanted. They knew only that there had to be a better way and they heard that Hyperion was a great product. In those cases, of course, we had to create a plan and provide a roadmap for them. But the real difference was that I helped them define the vision and a clear roadmap on how to get from where they were to the vision. I was also determined to transfer my knowledge and experience to them so they could begin to see how the technology could provide them with the solutions that helped transform their business including how to become more effective and efficient.

It then turned into a more collaborative conversation over time so that the customers were able to create better processes, new designs, and reports using more impactful data that would enable them to do their job better and to provide the company with more insightful reports. That's when it was fun and exciting. The student became the teacher and I began to learn from them. It added to my knowledge and abilities to deliver a more tailored solution to meet my customer's needs based on their type of business and industry in my future consulting. This led to my recognition that my success with customers was purely due to my focus on their needs, understanding what was impactful for them and what made their job easier and more effective at the operational level. I was putting myself into their shoes and asking questions about what I would want from a technology solution to make them more effective at their job and increase their company's ability to manage their performance more proactively and predictably to the targets. I understood their perspective, perception and expectations.

So why do I share this story with you? It is the lessons of these stories and the success that followed that empowered me to create the Customer Experience framework and a new, innovative approach that helps companies develop the best Customer Success strategy that will drive the outcomes and results that shoot them to the top of their market.

In my last few years with Hyperion, I was a Strategic Account Manager with a focus on the large strategic accounts like CoBank, Phelps Dodge, Safeway, American Express and many others. Our team mission was to manage multiple implementations of the Hyperion products across many customer teams and organizations. Again, I found myself asking the executive sponsors at these accounts a lot of "Why" type questions. It was vital to understand their business model, how they do business, what was working and not working, why were they looking for this type of solution, and what they expected the solution to do for the company. In other words, only after we understood their expectations, perceptions on what would make them more operational efficient and effective and what they defined as their success criteria could we determine what we had to deliver. By delivering to their perceptions, expectations and success criteria, we were developing a loyal relationship so that they would walk into their next executive or leadership meeting and rave about our solution that would optimize their ability to drive to results.

I'll never forget my first "Whiteboard" design session at one of my strategic account customers; CoBank in Colorado. I had representatives from the various departments that were interested in using the Hyperion products for financial reporting in the same room. The first part of the session was focused on asking them questions about how they operate and do their budgeting and financial reporting processes today. As they answered my questions about their operations, I began to draw workflows of their current processes and how they operated including how data flowed and what their expected outcomes needed to be to improve their effectiveness and efficiency. We also ended up with some nice diagrams of how they operated today that mapped out their processes and interactions with other groups. It showed many bottlenecks, duplicate information, and conflicts, which was interesting to many of the team members who were unaware of these issues.

The surprise came when the team members began asking each other more about the diagrams on the board. They began to edit my drawings and create their version of reality. But they didn't all agree. In fact, many team members were surprised by the reality of the workflows and how they actually operated. They were learning more about how their own company actually functioned and interacted. This discovery process helped the team to agree on where they were today and what the priorities should be for a Phase I solution to provide the most impactful benefits to the company. Want to guess how close it was to what was originally discovered in the sales cycle? Nowhere near what we had defined as their goals and success criteria during the sales cycle.

This process showed us how much we didn't understand about our customers, how they operated, what their priorities were, what their top problems were and what they expected as outcomes that would benefit them. We realized that we needed a better approach on our sales cycles to learning more about our customers to ensure that we had a clear line of site to their top problems and that we had the right solutions to solve these problems and how to present this in a manner that would resonate with the buyers and the teams that would be the main users. We modified our Discover phase in our sales cycle to ensure we had the right perception and understanding of our customers. The Sales team created a Strategy Workshop that was a modified version of our "Whiteboard" sessions and they drove the real plan and strategy we put in place for deploying the Hyperion products and the final solution that the customer's implemented. By setting the expectations correctly upfront in the sales cycle and by developing the right services program to ensure success, we were able to improve our "Time to Value" metric during the implementation stage of the customer's experience. It also enabled an expansion opportunity to come to fruition in a shorter time frame. Sales would then use this metric and the customer stories as references in their future sales cycles.

This real-life story illustrates how the focus on the customer's success with our solution drove more than just the implementation strategy or methodology. It also drove changes in the sales approach and eventually the product roadmap. The residual effect was that these customer's were all top references for us. One of the best compliments these customers would say about us was: *"Your team listens to our problems and difficulties and helps us strategize the best way to solve these problems with your solution."* They saw us as a team, not just a sales person selling a product and tossing it to a consultant to implement something that may or may not work for them. They achieved the benefits of the teams working together with the best interests of the customer in mind.

A CUSTOMER FOCUS THAT CREATES DYNAMIC FIRST IMPRESSIONS

An intense customer focus from the sales and services implementation and support teams provides a powerful first impact the customer experiences with your company in addition to the marketing events that draw them in as a prospect. As we all know, you must actually deliver on the promises that you market and sell. In other words, set expectations correctly and then deliver on them so that the customer believes that they have received every bit of the value you sold them.

So what role do your other company organizations play in the customer's experience to optimize the customer's long-term relationship with your company?

Other organizations in your company have plenty of opportunities to improve the customer's experience and the perception of your company, its products, and services.

The Marketing organization is an obvious example. They create the look and feel of the company and the products using various marketing tactics. This is often the first experience the customer has with your company. Marketing can quickly make or break a customer's interest in your company. This is primarily associated with how easy it was to understand quickly who you are, what you offer, and how can you help them solve critical or high priority problems.

Typically customers go looking for technology to solve a problem that is big enough to warrant a serious search for a solution. In some cases, you may have a product that solves a problem they don't know they have. In those cases, you would want to make it easy for them to quickly understand how they benefit from what you solve and how you solve it. The experience you are trying to create in this case is to intrigue them enough to contact you for more information. Thus, the marketing experience you design creates high quality lead generation.

Creating a customer experience that creates a dynamic first impression enables customers to form a positive opinion about your company. In my experience with Cognos, Ascential, IBM, and WorkFront, I spent time each quarter doing customer tours within each region worldwide. After creating a list of customers that represented each of our target markets and different company sizes, I would schedule a quarterly tour. During each customer session, I would typically learn about their experience with our marketing, sales, consulting, education, support, and customer success programs.

During one of these tours with Cognos, I was presenting our Corporate Performance Management solution to a new prospect with the sales team. I had incorporated a mini whiteboard session into my presentation in which I had drawn a vision on the board of how our solution would solve some of their top challenges and asked the prospective team for consensus. When I was done and asked the team if they felt this was the right solution and vision for their company, the CFO said, *"You should put that drawing on your website and tell the story just like that. The marketing webinar and website make it sound like your business intelligence solution and budgeting and forecasting solution are two different solutions. You made it all come together for us."* For the CFO, that drawing was the hook. Many marketing tactics can be great hooks, but the test is: Do the prospects and current customers perceive the information the way you think they do?

How many marketing departments take their marketing materials and campaigns out to current customers and ask the question: *"What is your perception of this new campaign, these materials or this presentation?"* It is always valuable to get a perspective from a cross section of your target market that have never heard of you or your products along with current customers who know you. You might find some messages and images that provide the right perception and are easily consumed to both audiences or that one audience gets it more easily than another.

EVERY DEPARTMENT CAN MAKE A DIFFERENCE IN CREATING LOYAL CUSTOMERS

As a leader in many high tech companies, I have learned the genuine value of supporting a customer experience as part of an end-to-end Customer Life Cycle model. As I describe in detail later in the book, this approach requires every organization within a company to play a role in bringing a new customer on board and in providing vital information to support them long term.

In any customer's life cycle journey with your company, one of the key processes customers have to complete with your company is the actual business transaction. The main organization involved in executing and supporting the business transactions is the Finance team that usually has an accounting, finance, and legal group. Sometimes, we don't think about the customer's interaction with these Finance folks when they decide to buy and continue to buy from you. However, it can impact the prospect's decision to buy or the customer's decision to stay with you based on how well they are treated and how easy it was to conduct business with you.

A major goal when I was with WorkFront (which was a SaaS Work Management solution) was determining how Finance could help us simplify our processes from sales to service to ongoing support and renewals.

For example, this included the process for negotiating a contract's terms and conditions, the process for invoicing and payment options, as well as the continued billing for services and purchasing additional products and services over time. We worked together with Finance to create the easiest ways possible for the customer to do business with us. Although challenging at times, we found many ways to keep the complexity behind the scenes and make the customer experience smoother so that it was easy for them to complete their business transactions with us while protecting the company with clear executable contracts.

WHAT IS A TYPICAL CUSTOMER LIFECYCLE?

The customer's lifecycle continually evolves. The customer starts with being intrigued by the marketing tactics, then are led through an evaluation process with a sales representative and product experts. Once the customer is ready to make a decision they will work with finance team members to complete their purchase of the solution. Now that they own the product they may require help with learning about the product and implementing the solution. This is usually executed by an education and consulting team to help customers achieve the right level of knowledge transfer and ownership to be successful. The services team goal is to create a baseline implementation that creates a solid starting point for the indispensable use of your solution. The services team will generally provide a strategic roadmap with multiple phases recommended for the customer to continue their evolution and maturity with the solution. The implementation team can then hand off this plan to an Account Manager or Customer Success Manager for them to continue to execute a Customer Success Plan with the customer team.

Customer success is maximized in these types of solutions by creating a formalized implementation approach that creates a detailed roadmap for the customer to follow. These methodologies would include following a traditional set of stages (i.e. Plan, Design, Build, Test, Deploy, etc.). This approach provides a set of tasks and deliverables at each stage to explain what is expected of the customer's team and what the customer can expect to be delivered by your implementation team. In essence, it becomes their plan for implementation and can be used to define a statement of work with a predefined scope of work.

THE VALUE OF A CLEAR CUSTOMER PLAN

One of my favorite customers during my Cognos days was a leader in athletic apparel. They were one of the first prospects for which we used our new Cognos implementation methodology to deploy our Finance solution. In reviewing the statement of work with the client's CFO, (which laid out each stage of our methodology with the list of tasks and deliverables by each stage of the methodology), his comment was, *"This is so simple to understand exactly what your teams are going to do for us and deliver to us for the price. I really don't have any changes. Most of the vendors we've worked with don't provide this much information."* In fact, clarity in what we were going to deliver and how created one of the best customer experiences the CFO had experienced with any vendor.

STANDARDIZING YOUR CUSTOMER IMPLEMENTATION APPROACH

To create a consistent customer approach, you should invest in standardizing your implementation approach and certifying your team to ensure every customer receives the same experience, similar to the story with the CFO above. At Cognos and Workfront, we invested in an internal education program to certify our consultants on our new methodology. This ensured that we had a consistent, repeatable approach, which would produce quality and excellence in our delivery for every customer. The consulting team that worked through the implementation with each customer also provided feedback to the management team on a regular basis. As they were using this new methodology, the consultants stated that it made it easier for them to provide a clear roadmap plan to the customer and to deliver consistent progress reports. One of our successful consultants on this team told me that he loved how the communication plan in the methodology allowed for the services team to determine the customer's perception of how they were doing. It helped him to compare their perception to his own perception of how they thought they were doing. He commented that the implementation check in sessions revealed some miscommunications and misperceptions from the customer team that the consultants could correct quickly to keep the customer team moving forward. In this approach, the services team provided a positive experience for the customer team and the many end users who would be our future champions and evangelists.

HOW DOES THE PRODUCT TEAM CONTRIBUTE TO THE CUSTOMER LIFECYCLE?

Even during implementation, the customer will face issues with the product. At this point, the customer is being introduced to your company's product team. Up to this point, the customer had worked with Marketing, Sales, Services, and Finance along their customer life cycle experience with you. Now, let's consider how the product team can positively influence a customer's experience.

When you think about the product team it may seem obvious that the customer expects the product team to make the product better and continue to innovate. However, we all know that no product is perfect, especially in the high tech industry. Bugs are the customer's number one area of concern. And they expect quick and complete bug fixes. I experimented with several approaches to improving customer communications in the face of product bugs to ensure that we understood the problem from the get go and then used technology more effectively to communicate progress and final resolutions.

At WorkFront, one of the most helpful tactics we implemented was the idea of a *'way forward'* solution. You might think of this as a work around solution to meet their needs without impacting the business until the bug fix could be generally released.

In the old days of all perpetual software, we would solve these types of problems with a "hot site" fix. It was technically a temporary solution to solve their one issue quickly. The product team then worked on the real solution that could be a part of the next main release. In some cases, the solution was actually tailored to solve a specific issue that was unique to them. However, in today's world of SaaS solutions, the notion of a "hot site" fix is not an operationally efficient way to solve customer problems even if they are unique to them.

So the WorkFront customer support team developed a methodology to find a way forward when customers discovered a bug that impacted their use of the solution. Sometimes this was a collaboration between our support team and the consultants to find a new configuration or design that would provide a similar result that was good enough to keep the customer moving forward with their day-to-day use of the solution. This gave the product team the time to develop the complete resolution and to release a higher quality product to the general customer base.

The product organization has a tough responsibility to the customer because they can't just stop working on the product release cycles in order to fix unique bugs. They have to work through a best practice methodology (i.e. Agile, Kanban, etc.) to provide the highest quality product in a timely manner. However, they are responsible for correcting bugs that do end up in the generally released versions of the software. From the customer's perspective they would like ALL of these fixed immediately. So how can the product team contribute to the customer's success?

AN EXAMPLE OF HOW EFFECTIVE THE "WAY FORWARD" APPROACH WORKS WITH CUSTOMERS

One of our largest customers was a top marketing service firm who was using WorkFront in a fairly complex manner. As I described earlier, I was meeting with them as part of my quarterly customer tours. After a lengthy discussion around the good news of how Workfront has been a valuable solution, we began going through their list of concerns. As expected, their top agenda item was to discuss their open issues of confirmed bugs. They needed to know when they were going to be fixed. My usual plan would have been to go through the list and try to determine which ones were production critical and basically getting a priority assigned to the list. However, I found myself asking questions about how they would like to see us provide information regarding their open issues. I asked: *"What would be most helpful for you to know to help you move forward with your use and expansion of the solution?"* The answer was surprising. They didn't say, *"Just fix them all."*, Instead, they made a simple request that we provide more insight into whether the problems would really be fixed and, if so, provide an estimated timeline, even if it was defined as late in the third quarter or next year. The issue was that the current status would always show "in progress" even if the product team never intended to fix it. They simply wanted transparency from us to be honest and state that it would not be fixed. In some cases, it was because the future product we were designing was going to do what they wanted in a very different way. The customer's response once I told them that was *"Great!, Just tell us that."*

What I learned from many other customers in similar situations was that they wanted enough information so their teams could make decisions on how they would continue their own progression and evolution of the use of the solution. It was very valuable to know where the product was headed from an innovation and roadmap perspective. This kind of information and feedback from our customers was vital to helping us make critical changes in our own backend processes to do a much better job of providing this information from our product team through our services team to the customer.

There was another concern that popped up during these customer tours related to our product information. The customers called it "The element of surprise." The customers loved the ability of a SaaS solution to provide continuous updates and innovations at a more rapid pace, however, sometimes the experience they had was one of "surprise".

They would log into our solution and begin to use it as they normally would. And suddenly everything was in a different place or didn't work as expected. This could be very frustrating, especially if they were under some deadlines and trying to get things done quickly. The request from the customers was for us to provide a "heads up" when any material changes were coming. This triggered some new processes and the use of our community website to provide more robust advance information. We also created a sandbox testing area for the customers to visit anytime and view the updated release using their database and review the changes that would be going live in the next few days. For larger customers, this was very helpful in their preparations, planning, and communications to their teams of any changes that they would be experiencing with the solution.

The moral of that story is that the customer's experience improved significantly because the services and product teams worked together on these solutions and processes to create better content, timing, and accessibility to the information in a more interactive manner. We focused on a solid communication plan to provide as much information in a more transparent approach to help them plan better for their future uses of the solution. We understood the customer's perception of our product quality and ability to provide good information in a timely manner. As a team, we then created a process to improve the customer's experience by creating access to our product roadmap information and the priority and status of all of their issues, which allowed us to maintain a solid relationship and partnership.

These are all great examples of how a well-planned customer life cycle can iterate on an on-going basis to continuously improve content, accessibility, usability, standards, processes and procedures around the customer's experience to improve their perception of you. It's the experience they have and the use of your solutions in an indispensable way that creates their perception of customer success. That is the customer success pot of gold that you are trying to attain in order to execute with quality and excellence in a consistent manner.

CUSTOMER ADOPTION CHALLENGES

Once a customer is using your products or services as part of their day-to-day activities and operations, they begin to realize the value of your solution to improving their effectiveness. The next logical customer process is verifying they experience real value that will continue long term. But a major challenge after the solution is in production is to get key team members to adopt the solution on a broad basis so that measurable value is achieved. Most customers will perceive short-term value from a production solution, but it is usually within a small group or team. However, the team using the solution in production needs to get additional groups and teams using the solution in order to benefit from more robust capabilities, improved information or processes. Getting to a fully adopted solution is where the customer's ROI is.

Adoption of any solution has been the number one roadblock topic for a customer to getting the solution embedded into their operational effectiveness and realizing the value and ROI. In order to address this concern, I started asking more probing questions around this topic:

- Do we understand how the customer team operates today and how they use the solution to do their job?

- What did they believe was the issue or roadblock for the teams to adopt?

- Did they observe a pattern, for example, a particular role or type of group?

- Did they ask the team members specifically what their challenges or difficulties were with using the solution?

- Did they feel all of their team members had the right level of education on how to use the solution to meet their needs?

- What were the most difficult areas for them to use and why?

- Did they have internal challenges in making needed transformation changes within their organizations to get to a more innovative state?

- Do we understand how to map a better way for the team to be more effective and efficient with the solution?

Most of the customers had no answers other than their own impressions of what they thought were the issues. Researching further we learned that most end users didn't know how to use the new solution as part of their day to day job nor how it would improve their effectiveness. They saw the solution as just another application and bothersome new system to learn. If they ignored it, perhaps it would go away.

While evolving the WorkFront implementation methodology, the issue of adoption came up early in my customer tours and was a hot topic at our user conferences as well. We conducted brainstorming sessions on how we can incorporate an approach within our deployment stage of our methodology to get enthusiastic user buy in on how the solution was going to make their job more effective and/or efficient. We needed to include a marketing message in our education program so that our clients fully understood *"What's in it for them."* We had to teach them how the solution would benefit them individually as well as creating value for their teams and for the company.

For example, our consultants would schedule one on one sessions with the various roles and teams to learn how they accomplish their basic tasks, processes or reporting in their current environment. We would then show them a better, quicker, more effective way to accomplish the same task, process or report using our solution. As we rolled this new approach out and asked for feedback on how well it was working, their overwhelming response was that it was the key to their successful roll out. The ROIs and value from the solution came to fruition much quicker as well.

These customers were also better positioned for their expanded use of the solution so we could begin planning the next phase of implementation. It was a very natural evolution for these customers and their experience, which contributed toward their loyalty. The customer feedback on my next customer tour with these customers, who benefited from our new approach, was one of a true partnership. The comments were *"Your team genuinely cared about helping us realize our success;" "Your team went above and beyond with every user to make sure they got it,"* and *"Your staff exuded passion and excitement which was contagious".*

At this point, you are beginning to see the trend behind making the customer's perception your reality in every aspect of your organization's approach to providing your target market with the best quality product and/or service. When you focus on meeting customers' needs in order to transform their ability to excel in their own markets, you create a relationship and partnership that endures long term. If you check in often with your customers to evaluate their perception of your company, product, and services, it enables your teams the opportunity to course correct and create an experience that nurtures and enhances your relationship and partnership. Do the right thing for the customer and everything else will fall into place. This customer-centric approach has contributed to the growth of the many software companies I have worked for over the years.

The following chapters offer a detailed and structured guide for you and your teams to utilize as a roadmap to follow to help transform your company into a customer-focused company. It is the approach your company takes in serving customers from the beginning of the customer life cycle through a continuous, easy to follow roadmap that creates an innovative partnership that ensures the ultimate success for your customers.

It will detail the Customer Experience Framework and models that I have used as a guide to helping each high tech company and my clients to create their own unique Customer Life Cycle model and approach by market to creating customer success.

Your teams will utilize this guide to help them define what success looks like for each of your market segments. That includes defining the right methodology for implementation and determining the outcomes and deliverables that create a customer for life. A Customer for life is one that has experienced high adoption and usage of your product along with a high indispensability factor. You will learn more about these topics in more detail as your work through the rest of the guide.

As you create your own Customer Life Cycle model, just keep playing the role of the customer at every point in the processes that touch your customers. By putting yourself in the shoes of your customer, you will see how they might perceive your company, its products, and its processes. You will understand how quickly and easily they understand what you do, what value you provide, and how you can solve their problem better than anyone else on the market.

Your own customized Customer Life Cycle will become your corporate way of life in developing and nurturing your customer relationship. It will be your organizational team's guide to how to serve and enable success with the various customers within each market. It will drive all your employees to see the customer's perception as your reality and find better ways to provide those customers with a transformational experience with your company and generate long-term loyalty.

CHAPTER 2
THE CUSTOMER EXPERIENCE MODEL FRAMEWORK

THE CX FRAMEWORK

A CX framework is a comprehensive model that not only incorporates the typical customer experience theories, but also provides a proven executable plan to deliver excellent results for both the company and their customers. The CX framework:

- Puts the customer at the very center of their operational plan.
- Takes into consideration all the touch points a customer engages with a company from inception to the ongoing long term relationship.
- Creates a companywide commitment to excellence in customer care.
- Makes it easy to do business with your company.
- Improves customer perception of your company compared to the competition.
- Differentiates you from your competitors in the market.
- Puts you in the thought leader position.

My experience executing this type of model for many of the top software companies today has taught me what works and what doesn't to optimize customer experience for various client types for each market segment. It makes customers understand that you really care about their success with your product and service.

One of the first companies who infused this type of model into their current approach to services was a financial reporting solution company, Hyperion. Their approach to services was to hire people with a financial background, teach them the software, and then send them out to the field to implement the solution once sales closed the deal. They offered a few courses they recommended a customer take and then it was up to the consultant to create the rest of the miracle. By changing the approach to a targeted model with a set of defined outcomes based on the type of customer and industry, we helped our customers find success with the solution using a best practice methodology. And we were able to increase the customer's ability to utilize the solution in a faster time frame showing an ROI in half the time from any of the competitors.

The framework for the CX model contains the following elements:

A Customer Experience Maturity Model
A Customer Experience Implementation Methodology that is used to develop, implement, and innovate the following elements:

- A Customer Lifecycle Model
- Customer Journey Maps
- Detailed Execution plan
- Customer Feedback
- Measurement and strategic pivots

The following chapters will provide the details on how to build, execute, and innovate these elements to allow your company to execute a CX way of life for your company as part of your future.

CHAPTER 3

THE CUSTOMER EXPERIENCE MATURITY MODEL

A Customer Experience Maturity Model is a model that describes the levels of evolution that a company will go through in their ability to create a loyal customer for life in a predictable manner.

The first element of the Customer Experience Model framework is the development of a ***Customer Experience Maturity Model***. This model comprises the stages of a company's "maturity" in terms of increasing performance predictability:

- **Ad hoc**: Basic survival mode with exception-based activity and no plan
- **Aware:** Project focused with a baseline plan and priorities established
- **Repeatable**: Customer lifecycle-focused with repeatable quality and finally
- **Predictable:** Customer outcome focused with collaborative innovation capability; quick pivot strategy

The model is important in helping a company define realistic expectations of their current capabilities to deliver a valuable customer experience that can create a customer for life. It also helps produce honest assessments of the company's current capacity to deliver the end result: a predictable approach to building a customer for life.

Figure 1 Customer Experience Maturity Model Roadmap

Customer Experience Evolution – Figure 1

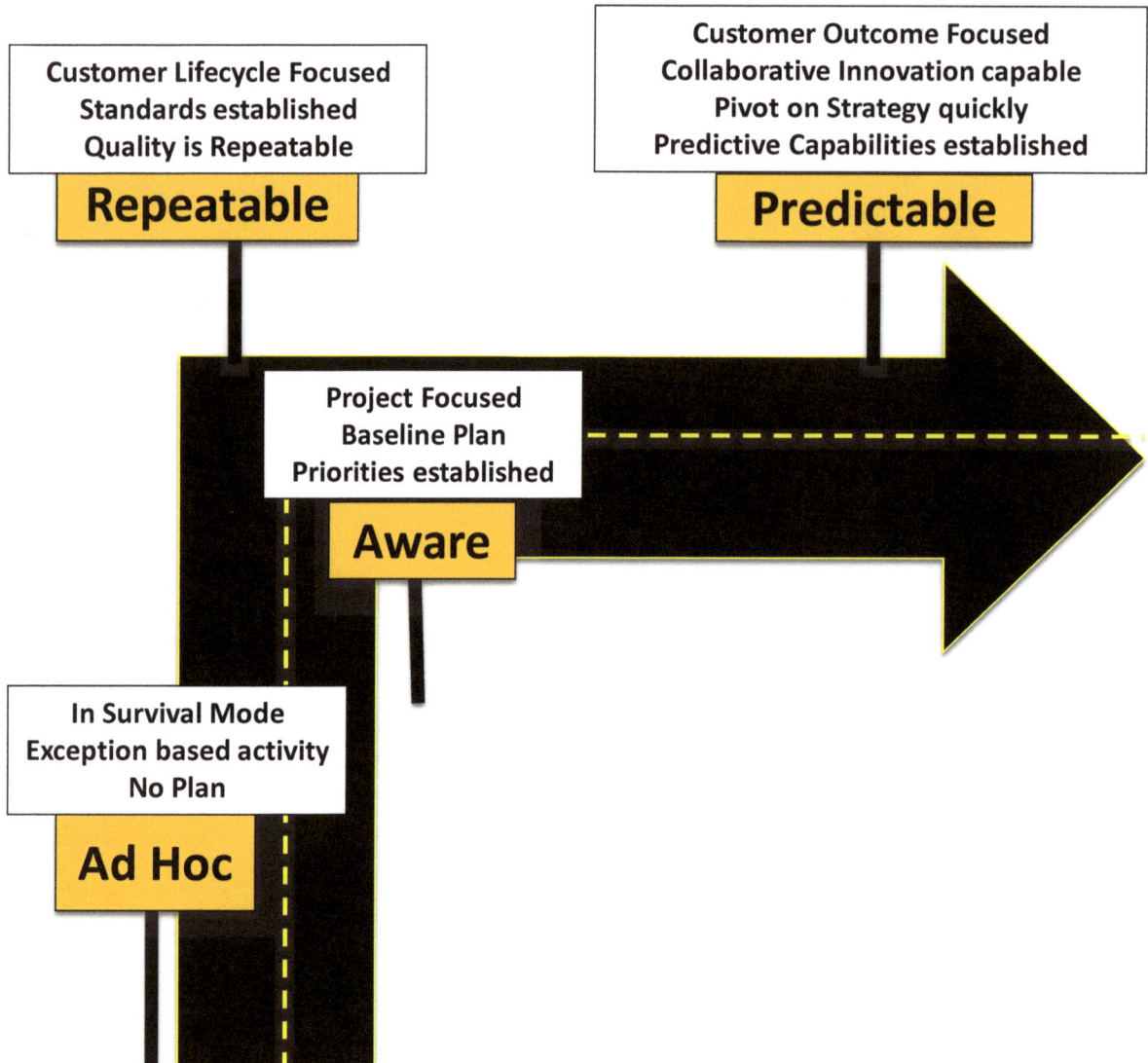

Customer Lifecycle Focused
Standards established
Quality is Repeatable

Repeatable

Customer Outcome Focused
Collaborative Innovation capable
Pivot on Strategy quickly
Predictive Capabilities established

Predictable

Project Focused
Baseline Plan
Priorities established

Aware

In Survival Mode
Exception based activity
No Plan

Ad Hoc

The ***Customer Experience Maturity Model*** will help you design a roadmap for getting from your current maturity level to the **Predictable** level to deliver the ultimate customer experience. It will allow you to determine what's needed to develop the essential foundation to deliver on new and improved standards, processes, procedures, and deliverables at an operational level. It will help you determine the level of reporting and monitoring required to measure progress that will enable you to pivot and make changes in an agile method. It will also show you the progression from survival mode to predictive mode. You will know when you achieve predictive mode because you will have control over your customer experience and be able to predict your quarterly outcomes within a range of 1% to 5%.

Each stage of the *Customer Experience Maturity Model* contains key attributes that describe the way in which you might be executing your customer's experience today.

Figure 2. Customer Experience Maturity Model

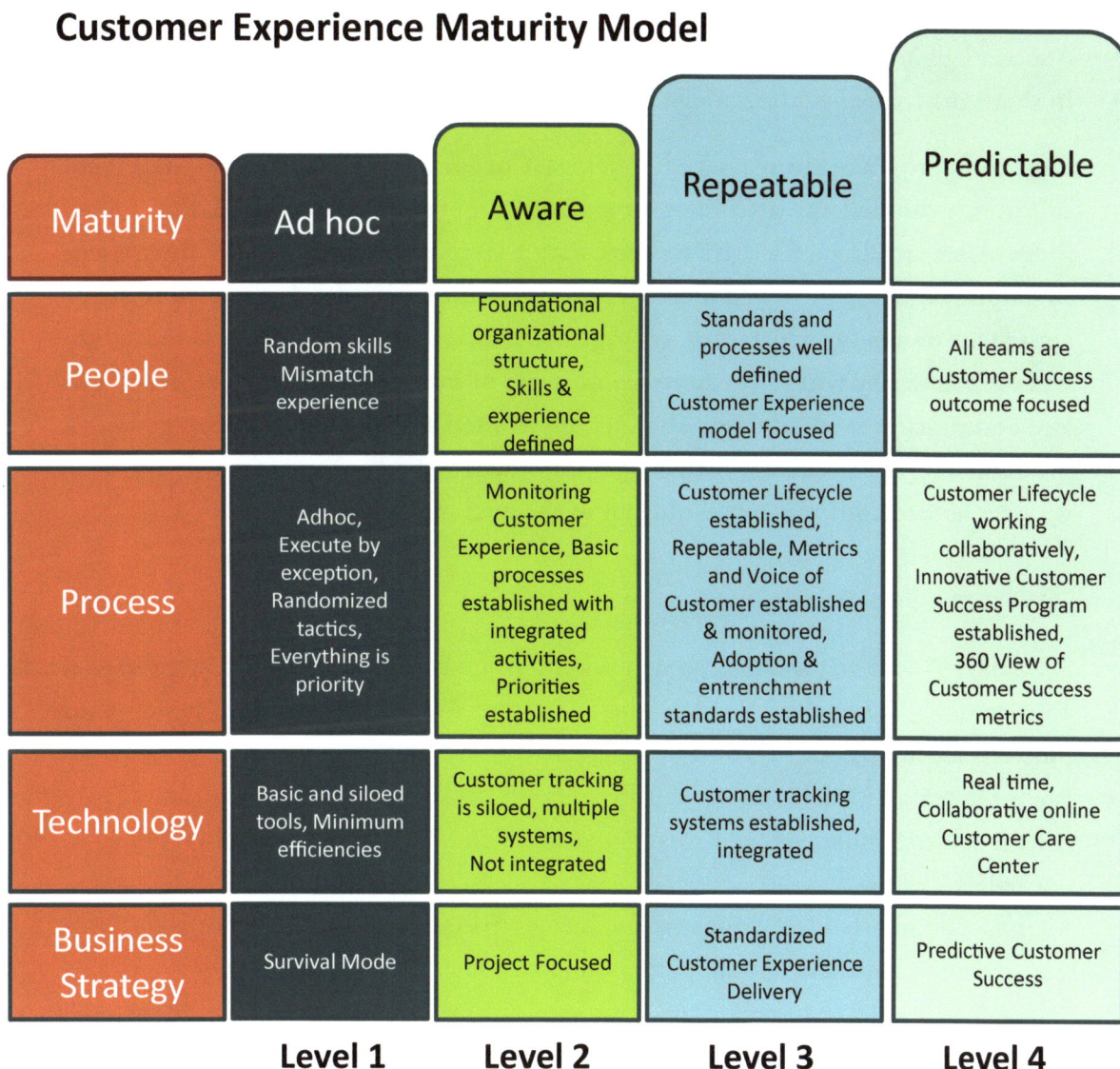

Customer Experience Maturity Model

Maturity	Ad hoc	Aware	Repeatable	Predictable
People	Random skills Mismatch experience	Foundational organizational structure, Skills & experience defined	Standards and processes well defined Customer Experience model focused	All teams are Customer Success outcome focused
Process	Adhoc, Execute by exception, Randomized tactics, Everything is priority	Monitoring Customer Experience, Basic processes established with integrated activities, Priorities established	Customer Lifecycle established, Repeatable, Metrics and Voice of Customer established & monitored, Adoption & entrenchment standards established	Customer Lifecycle working collaboratively, Innovative Customer Success Program established, 360 View of Customer Success metrics
Technology	Basic and siloed tools, Minimum efficiencies	Customer tracking is siloed, multiple systems, Not integrated	Customer tracking systems established, integrated	Real time, Collaborative online Customer Care Center
Business Strategy	Survival Mode	Project Focused	Standardized Customer Experience Delivery	Predictive Customer Success
	Level 1	Level 2	Level 3	Level 4

When you are at a level 1 maturity (Ad Hoc):

- The priority is usually the latest crisis, what is front and center or requests that come from the loudest people or customers.
- Your team is not organized according to processes, roles or responsibilities that follow best practice standards.
- Your company has not created or communicated its vision.
- Metrics or numbers drive the strategy. The customer is not yet your focus.
- A soccer ball mentality is in place; everyone is chasing the same ball.
- In short, the company is operating in survival mode.

One company, Workfront, which offers a Corporate Performance Management solution, exhibited the attributes of a Level 1 maturity level when I first joined them. After creating a basic framework with a simple methodology for their teams to follow, we were able to add more structure around the model that started to create consistent results in their customer implementations. This enabled us to move into a Level 2 maturity within the first two quarters of implementing the new standards and best practice methodology. The Customers sited that they were able to get quick productivity improvements with the solution using the new approach. From here, we were able to continue our evolution to the next maturity level.

When you are at a level 2 maturity (Aware):

- Priorities have evolved and are based on a basic vision and strategy to drive high-level metrics.
- Your team is organized with a structure to support the baseline strategy. Some standards and processes are in place to support the organizational operability.
- An Implementation methodology usually exists and drives the approach to customer engagements.
- A basic understanding exists of what works and doesn't. But this is not always documented or tracked.
- Metrics or numbers still drive the strategy. There is an increased awareness of customer importance. But strategy is not aligned to support a sound customer experience.
- Technologies begin to automate and track key processes, standards, and metric performance.
- At this level, a company is focused on project delivery.

At Workfront, we continued to evolve the model quarter over quarter. We began to track some key metrics around customer satisfaction, retention rates, expansion opportunities, and quality of delivery, usage, and adoption. They began to structure the organization to align around key target markets we more specific and focused go to market strategies. The customer feedback loop allowed us to begin iterating on our model and generate improvements in the customer value in a more standardized manner. We focused our customer outcomes to provide improvements in the customer's key metrics and optimizing operational efficiencies that lowered costs or increased revenue to get to real ROIs.

When you are at a level 3 maturity (Repeatable):

- The priority is process and quality delivery-centric, with a focus around delivering the best customer experience.
- Your team is organized, with a structure in place that supports a customer life cycle that ensures metrics are met and goals attained. Standards and processes support the customer life cycle delivery.
- You monitor and manage the performance of the customer life cycle using technology to automate and interpret what's working and not working.
- Customer experience excellence and value drive the strategy.
- You analyze and pivot as needed on the strategy and initiatives to ensure continuous improvement in the customer life cycle model.
- At this level, the company is focused on best-practice customer experience delivery.

As we evolved the maturity levels at Workfront, we were able to develop additional valuable customer success criteria with documented soft and hard ROIs. The company was beginning to experience consistent, repeatable results in their sales and services metrics and revenue goals. We were able to pivot faster in response to market changes and enter new target markets with a proven model for selling the right solution with the right services programs that created consistent results of value, quality and excellence.

When you are at a level 4 maturity (Predictable):

- The priority is based on innovating and evolving the customer's experience that creates a customer for life consistently.
- The organizational structure is collaborative. It supports a customer life cycle that ensures customer value and experience standards are met every time.
- Technology automates the monitoring and feedback loops to report and monitor results in real time.
- Customer feedback drives changes.
- The customer life cycle delivery drives the growth strategy.
- You analyze and pivot as needed on the strategy and initiatives to ensure continuous improvement in customer experience.
- You can predict the results and pivot quickly to ensure customer's value is realized.
- At this level, the company is focused on a predictable customer experience delivery.

> **With a proven approach in sales and services aligned with marketing and product, the Workfront was able to duplicate the model into other vertical market segments and grow the business exponentially using the same model and tailoring it for the solution and market with predictable results.**

You may want to determine which level each organization has reached within your company. A customer experience model requires some level of collaboration and engagement from every organization in the company. This is an important concept to get across to your organizations for them to understand and support the journey they will be undertaking overtime as they go through the maturity levels.

CUSTOMER MATURITY MODEL RISK ASSESSMENT

Understanding your end game goals is vital with a Customer Experience Model framework. Only when you understand how the maturity levels of your company's Customer Experience Model affect the customer's perception of your delivery and product value, will you have the guidelines you need to develop the best Customer Life Cycle model.

Figure 3 Customer Experience Risk Assessment

Customer Success Risk Assessment – Figure 3

Indispensability

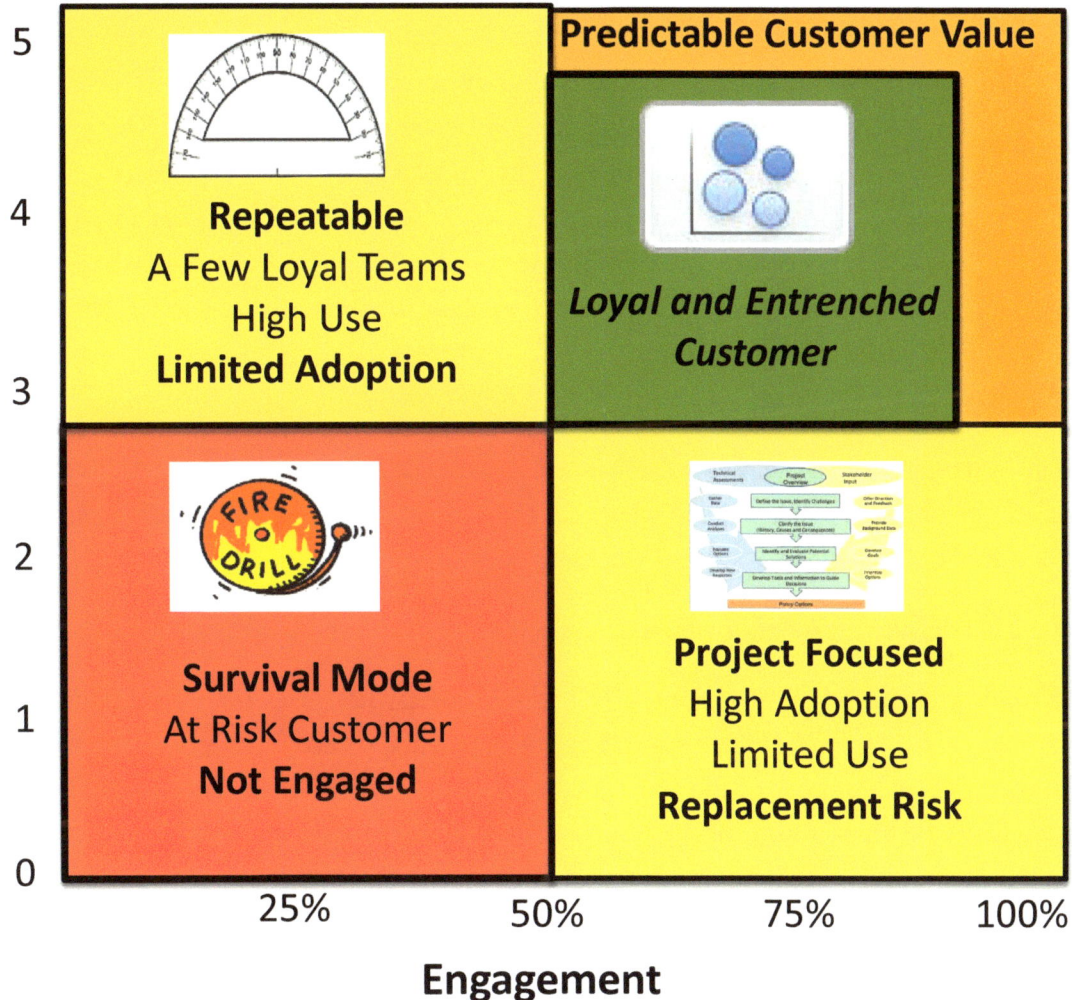

Two dynamics determine what type of customer your CX model framework will create; Engagement and Indispensability.

- Engagement represents the adoption rate the customer will realize at the end of the first round of your customer life cycle with your product. For example if the customer purchased 100 licenses and they have 100 active users fully engaged with using the product, they would have a 100% engagement rate.

- Indispensability represents the elements of the product being utilized that are critical to customer business needs and make it indispensable to the company in their daily operations or business. For example, when you have identified 3 key elements of your solution that are vital to your customer, they will be very unlikely to replace your solution with a competitor's solution. These elements can be functionality, process and/or integration to other systems.

It is vital to understand each of these quadrants. Every customer will fall into one of these quadrants. You will need to assess in which of these quadrants your customer fits. Once you have determined your customer's risk level, you can tag them as being in that particular quadrant in your CRM system and use it to help you assess the risky accounts in your customer base. Most Customer Success programs focus on moving your entire customer base into the green section (*Loyal and Entrenched* in your solution). However, the real goal is to get every customer to a Gold status where they are not just happy and using the product, but have found real value and a return on their investment to a level in which they will continue to invest in your solution long term.

Most of my clients in the high tech industry have found that their customer base landscape consists of around 50% of their clients in the yellow, 30% in the green, and 20% in the red. They have not created a status called Gold nor have they defined what that level of success is for their customers in each target market. They are not sure what real value is from their customer's perspective.

The following is a detailed explanation of the qualities that your customers will exhibit for each quadrant.

The Red Quadrant (aka Survival Mode) – This is the highest risk level. An example in this area is a customer that was sold 50 licenses for a few teams or groups to use; but only a few are using the software and in only a few areas of the functionality. It is not part of their daily, weekly or monthly work requirements for them to do their job or operate the company in any way. Your solution hasn't proven vital to their operations, lower costs, increase revenue streams nor improve their effectiveness in delivering their products or services. It is easily replaced with more than an 80% chance of churning and no expansion or continued future use.

The Yellow Quadrant (aka, Project focused or Repeatable) - This is the area of 50/50 risk. It means the customer can go either way with your solution. Some understand your value and some don't. However, many key influencers and decision makers believe your solution can provide some value but not the majority of key users that can advocate value or operational indispensability which leads to the risk of a 50/50 decision to replace or eliminate the solution.

- A Project Focused customer: they will have purchased the solution to solve a particular problem, issue or concern. It could be one big project or it can be in one particular functional area that your product works well for them. They are a customer who has purchased a high number of licenses (i.e. hundreds or thousands of licenses) and are using it for only one thing. It has a high adoption rate, but a very low indispensability rate. There is not enough traction with your solution into the company's operations where they see it as a must have solution to operate their business more efficiently and effectively.

- A Repeatable customer: They will have purchased dozens of licenses for use in multiple teams, but only one team is exhaustively using the solution. They use many functions of the solution. It is more entrenched in their day to day activities and is used to improve their job capabilities or the company's operations, however, they cannot get the other teams or groups to adopt the solution in the same manner. The solution has a dedicated champion and a few loyal users who see the value, but the organization as a whole doesn't see the solution's overall value and ROI.

The Green Quadrant – Loyal and Entrenched Customer. This is where most current customer success programs focus on to get all of their customers to a Green status. This customer was sold the right solution with the appropriate services programs and has the correct expectations for delivery from the very beginning. This customer has purchased 50 licenses and has all 50 licenses fully activated with multiple teams using at least 3 to 4 areas of the product. The teams find the solution indispensable to the company's daily, weekly and/or monthly activities for operating the business. It is impactful to their ability to deliver their own products and services to their customers so that they can grow and scale. This is a good healthy state for most customers to stay with your solution for the contract duration plus one renewal cycle.

The Gold Status – Value and Return on Investment (ROI). At this state, the customer has not only mastered and/or integrated your solution into their operational abilities, but they have experienced real value. The real value can be in the form of reduced costs, increased productivity, increased revenues, increase in market demand and/or market recognition for leadership and innovation. This level of value is the ultimate goal for creating customers for life. Customers are talking about your solution, referring you to other colleagues and companies and publicizing their success. This is the level you want to move all of your customers to for each focused target market area. The Gold standard level ensures customers have a multi-year plan in place for long term use of your product(s) and services.

With this understanding of the basic elements of a good Customer Experience model, there are a few activities that would be good for you to do with your team before you begin to build your CX model.

The first would be to have your company leadership team assess the maturity levels for each organization and set a goal for the company.

The second would be to have your company leadership team design and develop a Customer Lifecycle

Model for the company.

The third would be to set a realistic plan and timeline for building the Customer Experience framework. When built right, this framework will ensure your ability to predictably create and maintain Gold Status Customers for life.

Each subsequent phase of your plan increases your company's performance and capabilities as you mature through the levels. In developing your plan, I recommend using an implementation methodology to ensure your team follows a best practice approach to developing and implementing the elements of the Customer Experience framework.

The next section explains this implementation methodology. You will build an iterative plan that moves you through each phase of maturity. You'll also be constructing the elements of the **Customer Experience** framework defined at the beginning of this section.

CHAPTER 4

CUSTOMER EXPERIENCE IMPLEMENTATION METHODOLOGY

BUILD THE FOUNDATIONAL ELEMENTS FOR THE CX MODEL USING A CX IMPLEMENTATION METHODOLOGY.

A *Customer Experience* methodology enables your company to implement or update a Customer Experience framework. It creates a standardized approach that ensures a high quality delivery capability of the team to design, develop, and test the elements created within the CX model to ensure your company's ability to create Gold standard customers for life in a repeatable manner.

This methodology is designed to be a guide to the CX Committee or implementation team to complete a proper plan, design and implementation of their new Customer Lifecycle model. Once a you have a CX framework in place and have established your Customer Lifecycle model, standards, processes, procedures and policies, the team can continue to use this methodology to address new markets or major strategic plan shifts to evaluate and execute modifications.

Figure 4. Customer Experience Methodology Model

The Customer Experience Methodology – Figure 4

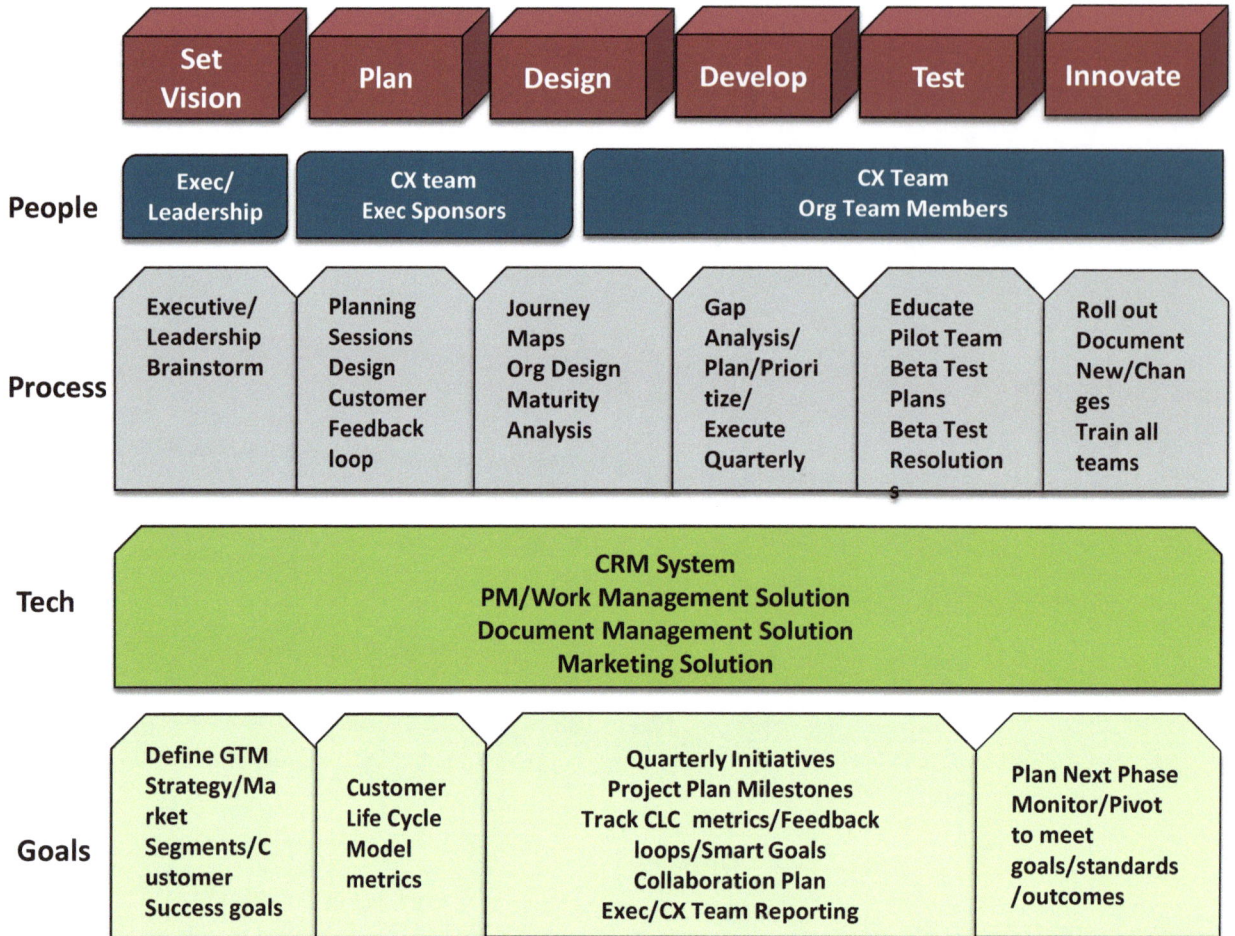

	Set Vision	Plan	Design	Develop	Test	Innovate
People	Exec/ Leadership	CX team Exec Sponsors	CX Team Org Team Members			
Process	Executive/ Leadership Brainstorm	Planning Sessions Design Customer Feedback loop	Journey Maps Org Design Maturity Analysis	Gap Analysis/ Plan/Priori tize/ Execute Quarterly	Educate Pilot Team Beta Test Plans Beta Test Resolution s	Roll out Document New/Chan ges Train all teams
Tech	CRM System PM/Work Management Solution Document Management Solution Marketing Solution					
Goals	Define GTM Strategy/Ma rket Segments/C ustomer Success goals	Customer Life Cycle Model metrics	Quarterly Initiatives Project Plan Milestones Track CLC metrics/Feedback loops/Smart Goals Collaboration Plan Exec/CX Team Reporting			Plan Next Phase Monitor/Pivot to meet goals/standards /outcomes

We will walk through each stage of the methodology in detail showing the elements the team will need to manage within each stage to create a quality customer experience approach.

Figure 5. Customer Experience Methodology

The Customer Experience Methodology – Figure 5

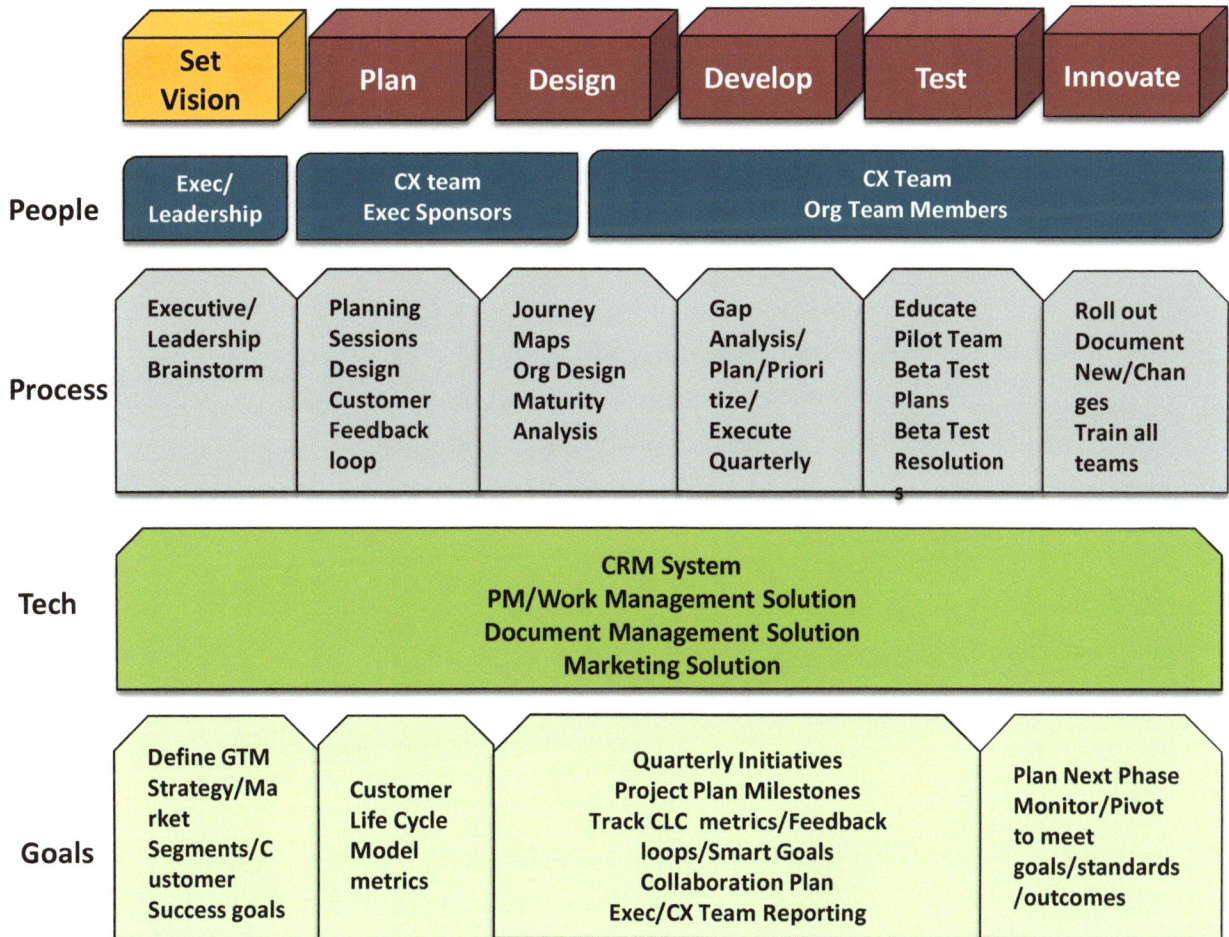

	Set Vision	Plan	Design	Develop	Test	Innovate
People	Exec/ Leadership	CX team Exec Sponsors		CX Team Org Team Members		
Process	Executive/ Leadership Brainstorm	Planning Sessions Design Customer Feedback loop	Journey Maps Org Design Maturity Analysis	Gap Analysis/ Plan/Priori tize/ Execute Quarterly s	Educate Pilot Team Beta Test Plans Beta Test Resolution	Roll out Document New/Chan ges Train all teams
Tech	CRM System PM/Work Management Solution Document Management Solution Marketing Solution					
Goals	Define GTM Strategy/Ma rket Segments/C ustomer Success goals	Customer Life Cycle Model metrics	Quarterly Initiatives Project Plan Milestones Track CLC metrics/Feedback loops/Smart Goals Collaboration Plan Exec/CX Team Reporting			Plan Next Phase Monitor/Pivot to meet goals/standards /outcomes

Purpose: Developing a vision for the customer experience model, starts by constructing a baseline *Customer Life Cycle Model*.

SETTING THE VISION

There are three elements that will need to be defined as part of your vision strategy and statement for your CX model:

    A. *Customer Experience Corporate Climate Shift*
    B. *A Customer Success Definition by Target Market Segment*
    C. *A Customer Life Cycle Model*

A Shift in Corporate Climate

Building a ***Customer Experience Framework*** embodies all things oriented to servicing and delivering a high quality, consistent, and valuable customer experience to all of your customers. This is a COMPANY WAY OF LIFE. It is not a group or organization within your company that you create and assign them the responsibility for customer success It is a commitment at the executive team level for all organizations in the company to do their part in contributing to ensuring the customer experience standards are always delivered from the first touch point through the on-going long term relationship. You will want to instill into all the teams the essential need to live and breathe a service-oriented approach and attitude. The company must truly believe that *the customer's perception is reality* and be committed to creating the perception that you are the best in the market.

Once you define your vision, you would market this internally to the entire company to begin the shift in the corporate climate so that the leadership for each organization promotes and includes a customer centric approach in their strategic plan. The leadership would then ensure that the core functionality of his or her organization is well defined as to how each team member's role contributes to the success for each customer.

With Workfront, I had to spend some time with the executive team to convince them that a shift to this new mindset within the company was a key success factor to transforming their company to a customer focused company. Originally, the executive team believed we could just create a customer success team that would deliver success for a customer. However, after reviewing current performance metrics and observing the decline in their results, I was able to convince them they needed to address customer success differently.

We were losing customers almost as fast as we were selling them. We needed to correct their churn rates. I pointed out that it is ten times harder to bounce back from a customer's bad experience then it is to get it right from the start. We had three different and unaligned playbooks running in the company between sales, services, and product. Our customers were being told three different stories depending on what group they talked with. Therefore, the customer never understood the vision that could create value for them in a clear and concise manner nor what implementation roadmap they should follow to find real ROI and success with the solution.

By aligning the company around a Customer Life Cycle approach, Workfront made the shift from a departmental execution strategy to an aligned company strategic plan with customer success at the center. The mission became focused on what creates valuable ROI for our customers within each market segment with all departments aligned around this new vision and focused strategy. The results were realized within a few quarters when customers provided feedback noting the changes they were experiencing with a more aligned focus on their needs and delivering products and services that were on point. They also noted that our messaging was now consistent across the various departments they worked with from Marketing, Sales, Services and Product.

Defining Customer Success by Target Market

Build your approach to serving customers by defining your North Star. What is a North Star? It is the definition of success the team develops internally for each market segment that defines what success is for the customers in that market segment. It's not what you and your team believe you deliver to the customer—it's all about how your customer perceives how and what you deliver as being valuable and creating a soft or hard ROI for their company or organization. It starts with the definition of value and/or ROI for the customer. Therefore, it's vital that you deliver to the customer exactly what they need to derive value from your solution so that you ensure high adoption and high indispensability (i.e. the gold section defined on the CX Risk Assessment diagram shown on page 33), which we will discuss in greater detail in the next chapter.

For example, at Cognos, our go to market strategy included verticals by industry (i.e. retail, finance, manufacturing, etc.). For each of these industries, we would define a specific implementation roadmap with outcomes defined that ensured success for that vertical based on the customer's definition of value and ROI that became their success criteria. The types of outcomes were designed to deliver the value in the form of the following:

- a set of reports for certain departments that were insightful reports that helped them to make decisions quicker that enabled them to drive to their end of quarter results in a predictable manner.
- Knowledge transfer to the key members of the department to ensure they could continue to create additional valuable reports and improve their analysis and predictive analytics capabilities.
- Design the solution so the customer team members were using all the key functionality aspects of the product as part of their day-to-day activities, by automating many manual processes. This lowered their headcount costs by improving the productivity and capacity of their teams.

- They would also define success criteria similar to the following examples:
  - Retail: Increase daily revenue by 15% by optimizing the floor design and product placements.
  - Financial Services: Increase profitability by 2% by managing cost decrease of 10% through process automation and reporting visibility from the top down.
  - Manufacturing: Lower cost of manufacturing of Product X by improving product quality and lowering defects by 5% through automated and real time reporting throughout the line.

There are several ways to develop your standards for what creates Customer Success:

- The Standard Approach ("The Rule"): The Rule is anything that meets the customer's needs 98% of the time. We know that we won't always hit 100%, but we want to shoot for creating value for ALL customers as our goal and allow for some margin of error. For example, the goal is for 10 out of 10 customers to have the following perceived success:
  - We've met all of the "Customer's Success Criteria."
  - The Customer is utilizing the product and highly engaged in 3 to 4 areas of the product's key functional areas that create the most customer value. We call this the Indispensability factor.
  - The customer feedback rated you high in quality of service and product value. (NPS, Customer Tour interviews, Customer Satisfaction surveys and/or Health Scores)
  - The customer believes the product and/or services are embedded in their way of life and improve the effectiveness of their job execution or overall operability and company performance.

  The Rule will form the basis for all your decisions for designing, developing, and executing your standard approach to your CX model.

- The Exception Approach ("The Exceptions to the Rule"): This is the flexibility you create within your standard approach. This is how you deal with the 5% margin of error. The processes you create to handle these exceptions are designed to change the customer's perception from bad to very good or excellent. The goal is to create approaches to handling these exceptions in way that still gets the customer to the success state you defined as indispensible and highly engaged. This will also ensure that you achieve your renewal and expansion opportunities and also preserve a long-term relationship with the customer.

Caution: Many companies get caught designing their customer success strategies and tactics around the Exception Approach. This leads to failure. I found it more successful to create your success definition around the Standard Approach (The Rule) and allow for flexibility in your approach to deal with any exceptions for those 'unique' customers. Even if you start out using the 80/20 rule to create your standard approach, that would provide you with a solid baseline to iterate and improve your capabilities over time as you mature, which will lead you to the 90/5 level of performance.

Developing standards means starting out on the right foot from the beginning. ***What you deliver in your customer experience in the first 30 days will drive the long-term relationship.***

A customer's perception can go from great to terrible in one experience if the negative impact is large enough. When it goes bad, you will spend ten times more time, money, and resources correcting the customer's perception from red to green and restoring trust.

Therefore, start from the beginning of the partnership to ensure that your customer always experiences something positive when engaging with your company at any level for any reason. It's best to build toward this vision, so that the exceptions you experience will be few and far between.

You can set a smart goal for your ***Phase I Customer Experience Model Implementation*** to have the results fall within the 80/20 rule as a start and then increase the goal by 5% per quarter (i.e. Q1: 80/20, Q2: 85/15, Q3: 90/10, etc.). The goal would be to have eight out of ten customers experience the rule and only two experience an exception. As long as you define a great experience for dealing with exceptions, you can restore trust quickly.

This would be a more realistic goal to give your team some breathing room to experiment with various ways to create the ultimate customer success without fear of failure. It will take time and experience with your customers to get a real understanding of what success looks and feels like for your customers. In other words, what the customer perceives as valuable, game- changing or transformative within their organization.

You need flexibility in your plan to experiment with ways to:

- Deliver your product and services
- Understand what Customer Success is by market segment
- Manage your processes
- Monitor results
- Report, innovate, and implement changes smoothly

Your organization can then evolve in its maturity and experience to deliver the type of customer success that changes their perception of your company and the value of your product and services.

With these concepts in mind, you can create a good baseline definition of what customer success should be for each target market.

For example, one of my client companies that delivers a master data management solution, began with three different products; one for data analysis, one for data cleansing, and one for data transformation. They struggled with finding success in delivering a Master Data management solution because they would sell and deliver each of the products independently. They sold a vision around Master Data Management and all the values it provides, but couldn't deliver on the value because of the segmented delivery approach.

Once the team understood the problem, they defined what success was for a Master Data Management solution for each of the market segments (i.e. Retail, Manufacturing, and Financial Services). They then transformed their entire implementation approach by aligning the product roadmap and implementation approach to eliminate one off solutions and customizations. Their new implementation approach provided a clear, well-defined roadmap with defined outcomes and deliverables that were confirmed as valuable and game changing for their organization. This approach generated a significant increase in average sales price per deal, shorter sales cycles, and shorter implementation time frames within two quarters of making the changes.

The Customer Life Cycle

The next step in building a vision plan for your CX model is to build a Customer Life Cycle Model for your company. A Customer Life Cycle model creates a collaborative customer centric approach to engaging with customers. You are building a new way of life for how you operate and deliver value to your customers as a holistic company-wide team. It takes a CX village to raise a customer for life. This is your master plan for your CX village.

A Customer Life Cycle model usually contains at least four sections. They can contain up to six sections depending on what you define as the start and end points for your CX model. For example, you might consider when a customer engages with your company through a marketing tactic as the starting point and the ending point when they renew and/or expand. Most companies consider the starting point once a prospect is qualified as a potential opportunity.

In a Customer Life Cycle Model, you're defining the sequential stages of the customer's engagement with your company from the beginning point all the way to becoming a customer for life. The following illustration is an example of a Customer Life Cycle model for a high tech company. In this example, The Life Cycle model is broken up into four sections called "Acquire," "Implement," "Value," and "Expand." However, your team will define their own lifecycle sections based on the product and services your company offers. These sections may be different based on Business Unit Verticals or Segmentation (i.e. Retail, Financial, Manufacturing, Healthcare, IT, Marketing, etc.) You should consider defining a different Customer Life Cycle Model for each business unit, vertical or defined market segment when the definition of what makes a customer successful in that market segment is significantly different.

A separate Life Cycle Model is required when the product and target market are different enough that the definition of customer success outcomes, the approach, offerings, deliverables, processes, and teams need to be unique in order to deliver the success criteria that was defined in the first step above. If the definition of customer success is different enough for each market segment, then the team should design a Customer Life Cycle Model specifically to ensure the success definition is delivered consistently and repeatedly with quality and excellence. In many cases, the Customer Life Cycle model will work for all target markets, but the approach required for the company to deliver specific success results for customers in the market require unique journey maps. We will discuss journey maps in Chapter 6.

Figure 6. Customer Life Cycle Model

The Customer Experience Methodology — Figure 6 Customer Lifecycle Model

A customers' first experience with your company usually begins with a marketing activity that draws the customer to your website. The examples used in this book assume we begin the life cycle from the point where a prospect drops into a potential sales cycle as a qualified opportunity. You can certainly start from the point where marketing is developing or nurturing potential prospects. You would simply add a section called "Qualify, Business Development, Account Development or Demand Generation" and map your processes around the development of your leads to qualified opportunities.

Therefore, first consider the sales, or Acquire, section, which goes from qualified opportunity through a sales process to a signed contract. Other names to consider for these sections can be "sell," "land," "evaluation," etc.

The second, or Implement, life cycle section begins with the initial implementation to the actual use of your product or service in production. This section generally involves the introduction of a larger implementation strategy and methodology. Other names to consider for this section are "Launch", or "Deployment". Timelines are irrelevant here. We are just considering the major elements the customer experiences throughout the Customer Life Cycle with your company. This section usually follows an implementation methodology of some kind that is included as part of this section.

The third section, "Value", takes the customer from simply using the product or service through the embedding of the product into corporate standards. It then becomes a way of life for the company where the customer utilizes your product or service as an integral part of how they operate their company and how they provide quality products and services to their customers. Thus they realize the value of your solution. This is the section where you validate the company's achievement of the original "success criteria" (the goals the customer expects to meet with the purchase of your product) and "stickiness" (what makes your product indispensable). This is usually the area where a Customer Success program is activated as a way of providing additional support, education, coaching, and consulting as needed to ensure they can entrench the product or service within their organization.

This section ends when a customer is convinced that your product or service is providing essential value to the company or organization and they are ready to expand.

In the final section, "Expand," the customer has already realized value from the product and/or service. They then want to continue as a customer and to discuss expanding the use of your product or service throughout the organization or company. Obviously, once the company engages with an expansion opportunity to purchase more product or services, the sales cycle begins again and moves through the customer life cycle model once more. Thus you have made a customer for life, who goes around your sections smoothly and enjoys the partnership with your company.

Figure 6. Customer Life Cycle Model

The Customer Experience Methodology — Figure 6 Customer Lifecycle Model

II. SETTING THE GOALS

You need to set goals for each section of the *Customer Life Cycle Model*. These should all align with your company goals and objectives both short-term and long-term. You will want to design your business intelligence dashboard to be able to monitor these goals from the top down in accordance with your go to market strategy.

The teams executing each section of the *Customer Life Cycle Model* must clearly understand the goals. I recommend that these goals are aligned to the company strategy and go to market strategy for each of the focused market segments. These goals are like bumper rails in bowling; they provide the team members with guardrails on how to measure, monitor, and adjust the processes, procedures or standards that will enable them to focus and execute successfully within the focused strategy. When the team comes up with a new idea or a change to existing standards, they'll evaluate them against the strategy in the focused market segment with these goals and ask themselves: "Does this allow us to achieve the goal better or is it a distraction with different goals that are outside our current strategic plan?"

A significant challenge will be reining in and controlling all the ideas and changes that arise during the process. The best approach is to build a Customer Experience Committee with representatives from all organizations in the company. This provides a control point for review and analysis. The team can also help determine impacts and implementation plans. The details of creating this team is discussed in the next chapter.

At Workfront, we developed a new Customer Life Cycle model. We did a great job at creating many new elements required for a baseline implementation of our Customer Life Cycle. We were able to get the basic elements for each section of our Customer Life Cycle model across the functional organizations in place with some feedback loops. However, we struggled in the beginning evaluating what was working and not working effectively. We enjoyed some great short-term results. However, it quickly became apparent that we needed to evolve the goals and a better mechanism for monitoring the results for each section, especially when the results were inconsistent.

- Why were some customers successful and others not?
- What was going wrong and where?

This is where the smart goals came into play. We established the bumper rails needed to keep us focused and better understand when, where, and how things were going in the wrong direction. Once we put the smart goals in place for each section with technology to track these goals, we found it much easier to determine where the inconsistencies were and what was causing them. We were then able to make adjustments easily and quicker to get the results more consistently in the customer experience.

Remember that your goals are all about creating the best customer experience which impact the key metrics that drive results. Don't fall into the trap of designing standards, processes, and procedures that support your model by making it easier for the internal company team members. This could end up delivering an inconsistent or poor customer experience. Too often members suggest changes that make their jobs easier or more lucrative, but don't improve the customer experience. The CX committee is the guardian of the process to ensure that your team takes a holistic view of the changes and validates that the changes improve the customer's experience and realized value.

Your goals should be challenging but achievable. Team members should be confident in their ability to deliver above and beyond their competition. Your customers should believe that you have delivered everything they need to succeed with your product or service. Remember "The Customer's Perception is your Reality". You always want to have an understanding from the customer's perspective when making changes to your business model. If you aren't sure what the customer would want, need or confirm is valuable to them with what you are proposing as the value propositions, then stop and take the time to do the market and customer research to validate.

Here are examples of various smart goals for each section of the life cycle model:

Acquire:

- Pipeline required to meet Sales Revenue target
- Sales Cycle time
- Success criteria defined by market segment
- Customer satisfaction rating for sales experience = 4/5 stars
- Average Sales Price (ASP)
- Win Rate

Implement:

- Internal service level agreements (SLAs)
  - Clear transition/introduction from sales to services within 3 days of close
  - Kick-off/planning Session within five days of close
  - Baseline use of product/service confirmed within 30 days of close
  - Customer implementation reporting is automated and visible to sales and services teams from Kick off.
  - Achievement of Support SLAs 100% per quarter
- Customer satisfaction rating for consulting/education courses and support delivery = 4/5 stars or >=98%
- All Customer Success Criteria has been met
- Time to Value (Time from contract close to Go-Live)
- Number of Customer Success Stories, case studies and quotes
- Number of Customer Go-Lives or Launches per quarter
- % Completion of Education Plan by Customer
- Average number of Support Issues by Severity per quarter
- Average number of consulting hours per customer to Go-Live by market segment

Value:

- Product NPS score > 70%
- Customer usage/engagement > 85% for active users
- Adoption % = 100% (i.e., if purchased 100 licenses, all 100 licenses are activated)
- Indispensability Factor is > 4 (This is the number of key product elements used by users daily, weekly, monthly as critical factors to their daily operations)
- Health Score (This is a mathematical calculation using multiple variables around usage, adoption, indispensability factors, rate of growth in ARR, number of users, type of users and other variables that are appropriate to understanding success for your solution. This establishes a score in which you have ranges for risk designated as Red, Yellow and Green)

Expand:

- Renewal rates > 90% (these can be defined by market segment)
- Expansion revenue => 40%
- Expansion Opportunity – within 6 or 9 months of Implementation start
- Predictability Metric (R/Y/G) (Risk Assessment metric)
- Total Customer Value $ average by Market Segment (Total Revenue $ potential of the customer)
- % Customer ARR to Total Customer Value

Once you have created a well-defined vision for your CX model, your team can begin planning for the execution of the model. This will require a proper implementation methodology for the team to follow to ensure that the elements of the Customer Life Cycle Model have a solid plan. The team should agree on the implementation of their new approach to creating a consistent customer success with proven results.

The CX framework has a proven methodology that works well for implementation of a customer centric way of life for the company. The methodology has five stages:

1. Plan
2. Design
3. Develop
4. Test
5. Innovate

CHAPTER 5

CX IMPLEMENTATION METHODOLOGY: THE PLAN STAGE

Purpose: To define the plan and the team for the development and launching of the Customer Lifecycle framework by phase

BUILDING A CUSTOMER EXPERIENCE TEAM

You need people on your team who believe in your vision for creating an end-to-end ultimate customer experience using your *Customer Life Cycle Model* as the guiding standard. Members of the team should represent each of the various functional areas of the company. A sample team would include members from the following groups:

- Sales
- Services (consulting, education, support, and customer success)
- Finance

- Product (a program manager, product marketing, QA)
- Marketing
- Distribution, if applicable.

51

Figure 7. Customer Experience Methodology: Plan Phase

The Customer Experience Methodology – Figure 7

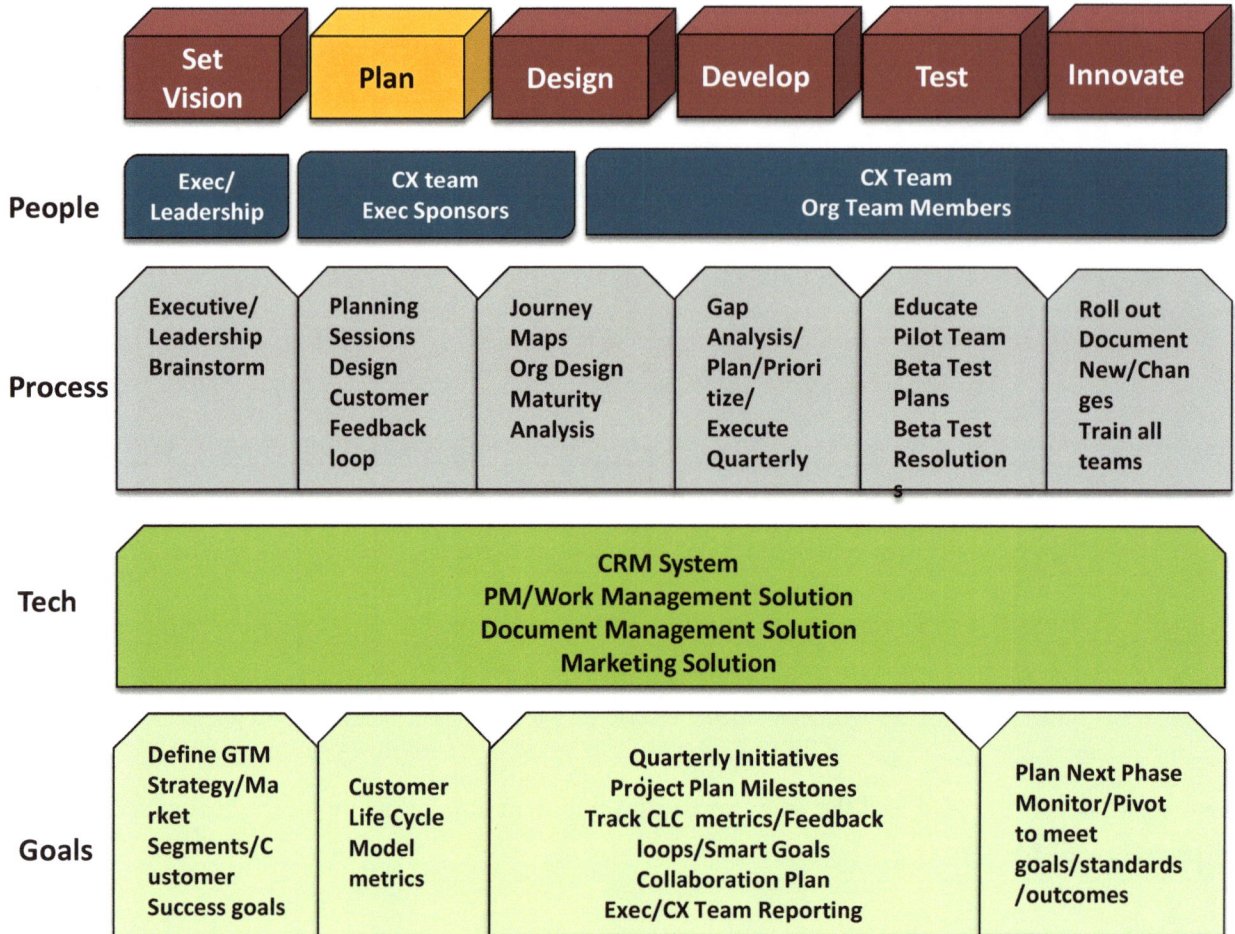

Set Vision	Plan	Design	Develop	Test	Innovate

People

Exec/ Leadership	CX team Exec Sponsors	CX Team Org Team Members			

Process

Executive/ Leadership Brainstorm	Planning Sessions Design Customer Feedback loop	Journey Maps Org Design Maturity Analysis	Gap Analysis/ Plan/Prioritize/ Execute Quarterly	Educate Pilot Team Beta Test Plans Beta Test Resolutions	Roll out Document New/Changes Train all teams

Tech

CRM System PM/Work Management Solution Document Management Solution Marketing Solution

Goals

Define GTM Strategy/Market Segments/Customer Success goals	Customer Life Cycle Model metrics	Quarterly Initiatives Project Plan Milestones Track CLC metrics/Feedback loops/Smart Goals Collaboration Plan Exec/CX Team Reporting		Plan Next Phase Monitor/Pivot to meet goals/standards /outcomes

The team goal is to build an experience roadmap that clearly defines how and why a customer engages with the company.

It's critical that the Customer Life Cycle Model should include all the touch points a customer has with the company. In fact, many other employees interface with customers in addition to customer support, product, consulting, education, customer success, and sales. Remember, it takes a village to raise customers right and keep them long term.

THE EXECUTIVE SPONSORS

Confirm that the Executive team members agree to be the sponsors. Their role is to lead the communication plan to the company to ensure that all employees understand the purpose of a customer life cycle and the importance to the company's strategy. The sponsors approve the required budget to develop, implement, and maintain the Customer Life Cycle as part of the company's way of life. This usually includes all the activities and head count required to implement and to maintain the model as the company matures.

As the CX Team evolves over time, it will present the overall plan annually for each phase, and the budget required, to the Executive Sponsors. As a pivot on the strategy is required from quarter to quarter, the team will present change requests based on the complexity, impacts, and costs of the change. Only those changes that exceed a certain budget or impact to the company should go to the Executive level for approval. The CX team should have members with authority to execute on more than 80% of the changes required in order for the team to fluidly iterate on the model. In most company structures, these can be incorporated as part of each of the departments strategic plans that aligned to the corporate strategy. Eventually, you may disband this committee as it becomes how you plan and execute as part of your annual and quarterly planning and performance evaluation processes.

Define the goals for Customer Life Cycle

The goals you define for the overall Customer Life Cycle should provide assurance that your customer is experiencing value and positive interactions with all company employees. These can be both high-level goals and also specific smart goals that measure various activities and programs.

Set up your goals by each section of the Customer Life Cycle. They are either an improvement to a current goal or a new goal defined to track a new program, activity or process and the outcomes from these. An improvement goal would be used when launching new programs or offerings or processes in which you expect an improvement in a current metric. A new goal would be a new metric that you are creating to provide insight into whether new elements or changes are working and making the impact on results that you expected.

Table 1. Examples of Improvement and New Goals:

Improvement targets:	New Goals:
Renewals improve by 5%	**Renewal Rate >= 90%**
SLA targets improve by 10%	**SLA targets =100%**
Number of Customer Service calls reduced by 15%	**Customer Service Severe Level 1 issues < 5/month**
Expansion leads increase by 10%	**Expansion lead Pipeline >= 2 times quota**
Sales Win Rate improves by 20%	**Services $/License $ % > 75%**
Customer Satisfaction rate increase by 3%	**Customer Satisfaction Goal >=95%**
New Product/Service offering improves product usage by 20%	**New Product/Service usage >= 80% for all active users**
Enterprise Account Engagement for current customers improves by 10%	**Enterprise Account Engagement score for new accounts > 80%**
Traffic on self-help website increases by 25%/quarter	**Customer Self Help Center website traffic >= 1000 views**
Time to Value improves by 1 week by end of each quarter	**Time to Value < 90 days**
NPS Score increase by 15%	**NPS Score >= 8**

Each section of the Customer Life Cycle will have a set of Metrics. The team will identify the goals from quarter to quarter for each metric and measure the results.

For Example:

The Acquire section would be measured based on the following metrics:

- Win Rate
- Sales Cycle days
- Average Sales Price (ASP) or Average Contract Value (ACV)
- Services $/License $ (%) (Initial sale)
- Qualified Lead conversion rate (%)
- Pipeline dollars available to meet quarterly target

The Implement section would be measured based on the following metrics:

- Time to Value
- Customer Satisfaction
- Adoption Rate
- Engagement Factor
- % Customer Success Criteria Met

The Value section would be measured based on the following metrics:

- Renewal Rate
- Usage Rate
- Adoption Rate
- Engagement %
- Indispensability Factor
- Customer Satisfaction or NPS score
- Average Customer Reference rating by segment
- Renewal Risk Factor
- Renewal Prediction %
- Customer ROI

The Expand section would be measured based on the following metrics:

- Customer Growth rate
- Revenue Growth rate
- Total Customer Value/Potential

The team would agree on the goals to set for each of these metrics. For those metrics that are new for the company, the team should track these for a quarter or two first and then set the appropriate target. For metrics that are currently being tracked, a new reasonable target should be set.

Define the Timeline and Key Milestones

The CX Leadership team should identify the summary level timeline for the Customer Life Cycle Model Implementation with key milestones.

The best approach is to implement the elements required to execute a baseline Customer Life Cycle for one market segment. Keeping the maturity model in mind, the iterations over time will evolve the Customer Life Cycle along the maturity model as well as the team's execution capabilities.

The Plan

The Customer Life Cycle model is an iterative execution plan. Therefore, the Customer Experience Team will always be planning the next phase of evolution as the company grows. The team will plan from quarter to quarter, modifying the plan as required in order to continue delivering on the company goals and objectives following the strategic plan.

I recommend using an online project management solution in order to manage the detailed plan collaboratively by quarter on the priorities and the required foundational elements needed to get to the next level of maturity. There are many options out there today, whether it be a (Software As A Service) SaaS or on premise solution. Based on your size and budget, I would do some research to find one that fits your needs with the capabilities required to manage your CX implementation and collaborative communication effectively. I personally like the SaaS solutions on the market today as they are cost effective with robust project management functionality and allow for worldwide collaboration if needed. At a minimum, the team should develop a summary-level plan with the priority elements identified by each Customer Life Cycle section that sets an implementation with quarterly target dates.

The Customer Experience Leadership Team should review the summary plan and provide their approval for the team members to begin building out the details for designing, developing, testing, and evolving over each quarter with targets clearly laid out to meet the annual goals.

With a summary plan defined, the team can begin setting up weekly or biweekly meetings with the CX team and move into the Design stage of the implementation methodology.

When I joined WorkFront , it was one of the smallest companies that I had ever worked for. As I began to put my plan together to build the foundational aspects of a new implementation model, I worked with the Sales and Services team. I spent time sharing the plan with the team members and getting their buy in and feedback. The key transformational elements to get them involved in making the changes was explaining how they would benefit individually, as a team, and as a company.

By developing a formalized plan, I could share the plan easily with the Executive team as well as the teams whose engagement and support I needed to execute in a timely manner. This was the first key step to successfully delivering the foundational elements within 90 days. Even the board was pleasantly surprised at the pace in which we were able to make the changes and impact the results.

CHAPTER 6
CX IMPLEMENTATION METHODOLOGY – THE DESIGN STAGE

Purpose: To design the detailed roadmap a customer will follow at each section of the Customer Life Cycle Model for each market segment.

The Customer Life Cycle roadmap evolves from the Customer Journey maps that are created for each section of the Life Cycle.

DEFINING CUSTOMER JOURNEY MAPS FOR EACH SECTION OF THE LIFE CYCLE MODEL

A customer journey map is a roadmap to the executable plan for each section of the Customer Life Cycle. These are critical because they provide the details for developing the ultimate customer experience for every touch the customer has with your company. At each section of the Customer Life Cycle, a customer journey map will define the process, standards, people and/or services a customer will experience every step of the way during that section of the partnership with your company. There are two kinds of customer journey maps:

- A current customer journey map, which is what you do today
- A visionary customer journey map, which is what you know a customer needs to experience to become a loyal, entrenched customer for life.

In this phase, the team will spend a few days or even weeks to brainstorm the right customer journey map for each section.

Figure 8. Customer Experience Methodology: Design Phase

The Customer Experience Methodology – Figure 8

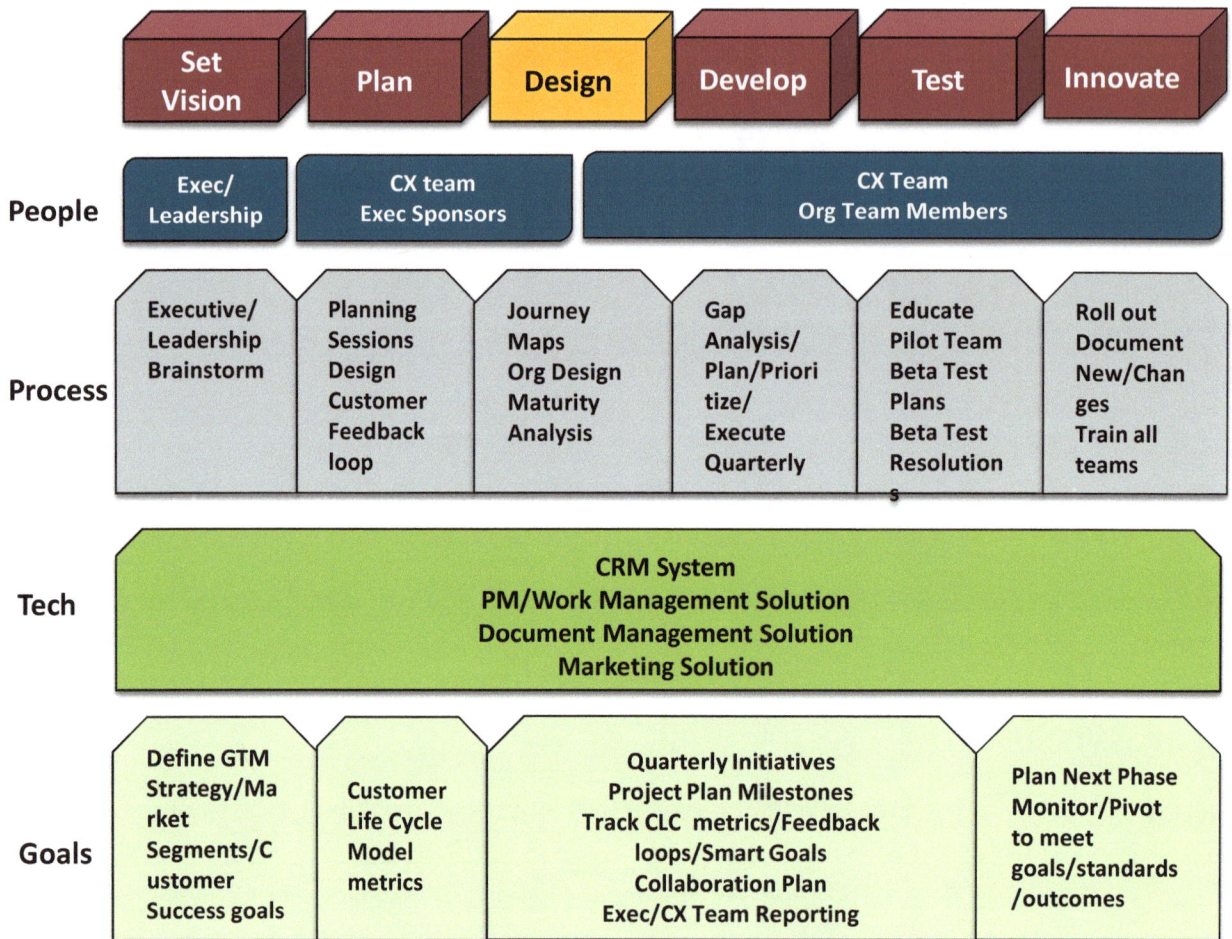

Set Vision	Plan	Design	Develop	Test	Innovate

People	Exec/ Leadership	CX team Exec Sponsors	CX Team Org Team Members		
Process	Executive/ Leadership Brainstorm	Planning Sessions Design Customer Feedback loop	Journey Maps Org Design Maturity Analysis	Gap Analysis/ Plan/Priori tize/ Execute Quarterly	Educate Pilot Team Beta Test Plans Beta Test Resolution s	Roll out Document New/Chan ges Train all teams
Tech	CRM System PM/Work Management Solution Document Management Solution Marketing Solution				
Goals	Define GTM Strategy/Ma rket Segments/C ustomer Success goals	Customer Life Cycle Model metrics	Quarterly Initiatives Project Plan Milestones Track CLC metrics/Feedback loops/Smart Goals Collaboration Plan Exec/CX Team Reporting		Plan Next Phase Monitor/Pivot to meet goals/standards /outcomes

The first step in preparing for your journey mapping sessions, is to research and organize the customer information for the market segment you will be tackling first. This information includes understanding the types of customers in the market segment, industries, departments and personas (i.e. buyers, influencers, sponsors, project managers, users, etc.). The next step will be to do some analysis on this information including using a select set of customers in this market segment that you can interview and validate what their experience has been and what they want and need to experience with a vendor as well as the ultimate ROI and customer success criteria required to renew and expand the use of your products and services.

In order to develop the details behind each section of the Customer Life Cycle, you will need several design session meetings. In many cases, you can schedule one meeting for each section. The goal of these meetings will be to define the details of all the various processes the company currently has, or may be missing today, in order to deliver the highest quality and consistent experience with your products and services within that section of the Customer Life Cycle. As you develop the customer journey map for each section, review your vision, goals, objectives, and metrics and discuss the following:

Put yourself in the Customer's place and play the role following the process(es):

- What are their challenges or problems that your product or service resolves?
- Who cares about these challenges?
- What impact could your solution have to my organization or business?
- What would success look like for their company or organization?
- What real value and ROIs do we have to deliver to create a long term commitment to our solution?
- How long should that take and what services do we have to provide to help the customer realize their success criteria?
- Review what the customer sees, hears, interacts and perceives throughout each process in the section you are mapping.
- What's missing in order to meet their expected success criteria and deliver the highest quality of excellence in that process or deliverable in a consistent manner?
- What is the customer's perception today of similar solutions?
- What's not working today? How would we improve that? What would that look like?
- How can we measure the success of the new process in order to evaluate monthly what's working and not working?
- How can we automate certain aspects of the execution of the process as well as monitor our effectiveness within this section?

In working with an Agile software solution client, it was interesting to work through this exercise with the team. The team's tendency was to tell me what they did today and talk about the one off exceptions that they encountered. They had a tough time articulating what the customer's needs were, what problems were we solving for them and what did they expect as an ROI or valuable outcome. This made it difficult to determine what they should do to optimize the customer's experience. That's because they weren't really sure what the customer was experiencing or what the customer's real value expectations were. Although they had some verbal feedback on a few cases, they hadn't collected any data on the customer's perception of their company, their processes, and their product value, even using the 80/20 rule. Remember the 80/20 rule is what 80% of the time the customer's would expect and require.

If you find yourself struggling with this exercise, I encourage you to go on a customer tour of a variety of customers in the various market segments in order to uncover their real perception of the various processes they have experienced from sales to implementation to support and to on-going service as well as find out what they expect from your type of solution and services. Find the most successful customers and document what their success criteria are and any ROI they have realized to date. This will add vital data points to the development of the visionary journey map.

THE SECRET SAUCE TO REAL CUSTOMER VALUE

The secret to building a solid foundation behind your customer experience model is to have a clear definition of what the customers in your target market view success as for their company. Is it operational efficiency or effectiveness, improvement in revenue generation, cost savings, organizational optimization, or other types of value specific to a niche market? I would suggest you spend the time with a variety of customers and prospects in your target market to collect a wide range of customer feedback and true perceptions and expectations of what they need from a solution to make it worth a long term and higher investment.

The approach that I have experienced works best at getting to a clear definition faster is to first select a group of customers that represent your most successful, long term or creative uses of your solution. These customers are usually the ones that you use as references, as part of the beta testing of new releases, speakers at your user conference or have continually expanded.

The second step is to schedule a 2 to 4 hour strategy workshop with each of these customers. The purpose of this workshop is to understand their business model, top strategic objectives at a company, organization and department level and learn how your solution has transformed or improved these organizations and key goals and objectives. The preparation for these workshops is to learn about the customer's business, competitive landscape and products and services they bring to the market. A whiteboard is best to use during the workshop to document the session.

The third step is to model out on the whiteboard the structure, workflows, processes and procedures they utilize today and where your solution has made the biggest impact. This is the start of identifying where the value and ROI is being generated for your customers. If they found value around processes, it is usually due to automations, better and faster information in the hands of people making decisions or decreasing time frames in delivering their products and services.

The fourth step is to try to quantify the value the customer has articulated during the workshop. If they can share the impacts in terms of improvements in key metrics that may have an impact on increase in revenues, reduction in costs and improvements in profitability, you can turn these into statements around realized value and ROI.

Once you have completed a dozen of these workshops from your target customer list, you can begin to collect this information into a database that you can analyze trends for your target market. This will be the information you will want to bring into your journey mapping sessions as the definition of the specific outcomes you want to build a standard experience and process for all customers to realize with quality and excellence in service in a repeatable manner.

When I was at WorkFront, I went on a quarterly customer tour. Each quarter, I would visit at least 5 customers that represented each of our market segments. We would spend a few hours together going through an agenda that included hearing from them on what was working well and what wasn't working well, the value they were realizing from the product and services, what they would like to see from us in the future and then ending the meeting by sharing the product roadmap and new services, offerings or changes that were coming in the near future. The best part of the meeting was asking the customer how we could serve them better. This customer information was critical to the changes and pivots we made in the future to continue to drive improvements in the customer's perception of our company and products. It helped us uncover what was needed to get them to the indispensible state in using our solution, which would enable further expansion opportunities. Many of the changes we implemented were not just in the product roadmap but also to the types, quality and delivery vehicles for services to help support our customer teams and all users.

Let's begin by going through an example of how to map out a customer journey, both current and visionary, for the Implement section, of the Customer Life Cycle Model.

You'll be defining your journey maps in sections, as defined here:

A. Map the current customer experience (in diagram format)

- Define the processes the customer goes through in each step along the flow for that section.
- Define the purpose of the process and benefit to customer.
- Identify key areas of customer concerns that impact success.
- Is there a metric that can be tracked for direct feedback on what's working or not for each process within each section?

B. Map a visionary customer experience (in diagram format)

- Define the Customer's buying process and the players involved.
- Define the Customer's team members and the problems the solution or services resolves for them.
- Define the Customer's success criteria based on their expectations
- Define the processes the customer would go through in each step along the flow for that section in order to meet their expectations and success criteria.
- Define the purpose of the process and benefit to customer.
- Is there a metric that can be tracked for direct feedback on what's working and what's not for each process within each section?
- Make sure you resolve any areas of concern or issues that the customer faces today in doing business with you easily and with clarity.
- Develop processes you can deliver consistently with quality and excellence.
- The goal of this map is to create the processes, standards, work flows, and people to ensure consistent execution of the customer success standard you defined in the plan/design stages in order to create a fully engaged and entrenched customer for that market segment.

C. Identify any gaps between the two

Are there differences between the visionary customer journey map and the current customer journey map? The team will be documenting the gaps within each stage to put together a strategic plan that can be executed quarterly over quarter.

D. Define the people and their roles

Know who is required to execute each process, monitor execution quality, review exceptions, monitor customer feedback loops, and evaluate what's working and what's not working on a regular basis. The roles should be defined with responsibilities and skill sets required to create quality and excellence for each process and section along the customer experience journey.

E. Set up customer feedback loops

Establish the feedback loops at various points in the process. Define teams to evaluate feedback data, make decisions on changes, and manage the implementation of changes. Remember the customer's perception is very important to understand what they consider value and ROI to be. Have you provided a real game-changing value to their organization or company with your solution? Do you know what that value and success criteria is for the majority of the customers you would sell to in the market?

F. Develop appropriate metrics and goals

These should be meaningful for the type of process, service and product being delivered that can be tracked as a smart goal. These can be made team goals and incorporated into a bonus plan to motivate the teams to generate the highest impact on the results.

Let's discuss each of the above elements in more detail since this is where the teams will spend most of their time in executing the Customer Life Cycle Model. The Customer Journey maps will be your design for that section of the Customer Life Cycle model. Once you have theses elements defined, you will be able to put your detailed execution plan together and kick-off the first Phase of the Customer Life Cycle Implementation.

A. Map Current Customer Experience Journey Maps (in diagram format)

I recommend using a large whiteboard; a room with multiple whiteboards would be ideal. You can always take pictures and document into a Visio-type technology later.

The team will start with the first section of the Customer Life Cycle model. For example, the first session you may schedule is for the Quality and Acquire sections which will define the Marketing strategies by each market segment and the tactics used to generate a pipeline of qualified opportunities for sales to work with each quarter to ensure they can hit their quota through the sales cycle to the close of a deal. In order to create a quality journey map the team should brainstorm on each step a customer goes through, from the time your customer is introduced to your company or one of your product or services, through the purchase process. In the follow up sessions you will continue the same brainstorming with the team and walk through the customer experience all the way through delivery, ongoing support and the expansion of your solution.

You'll want to evaluate the entire customer journey that your customers experience today and document this on one board or wall. This will include the definition of each component of the process that your customer experiences today in detail including all policies, standards, processes and procedures and the people accountable to executing and decision makers.

B. Map Visionary Customer Experience Journey Maps (in diagram format)

Once you have a map of what your customer journey is today and all the processes the customer experiences for the Customer Life Cycle section you are working on, you then can use another white board or wall to map the visionary journey map. The visionary journey map should reflect what you know about your target customer and current customers. It should be the definition of what the customer journey needs to look like to create a consistent outcome that delivers the value and ROI that you have discovered creates loyal and entrenched customers with your solution.

As you map the Visionary Customer Journey for a specific focused market segment, keep in mind the following goals:

a. Target market – A reminder that as you define what valuable outcomes are required to create long term success for this target market, you will be deciding if the requirements for this target market are so unique that you will need a separate Customer Life Cycle model for this specific target market. If it appears that the outcomes and success criteria required to create entrenched customers for this market are common across the various target markets, then you can start with one Customer Life cycle.

b. Customer Success Definition – From the Vision that was defined for your Customer Life Cycle (defined in the earlier chapter), you will have a clear definition of what a successful customer's outcomes and success criteria are to deliver real ROI and value to customers. This would lead you to understand how to build a set of roadmap goals and objectives that create an Entrenched and Loyal customer (green to gold quadrant of Risk Assessment diagram)

c. Key metrics targets – Think about the metrics that you want to put in place to track the progress of your execution abilities and consistency in delivery throughout each section of your Customer Life Cycle.

d. Transition – Spend the time to discuss and define how you will transition customers from one experience to another, which usually involved transition from one department that owns a process to another or from one team to another.

e. Organizational structure impact – Your new visionary journey map may require the team to review with the Executive team ideas for improving the organizational structure to make it more effective for the team to provide a better customer experience. Don't get stuck in designing standards and processes around how you are organized today as it may require considerable changes to deliver according to your new vision.

The secret to the model is to develop smooth transitions from one section to another as they continue their long-term relationship with your company. Transitions throughout the Customer Life Cycle model have significant impact on the customer's perception of your company. This may be in the sales to service transition, in expanding the use of your products or in purchasing new products or services.

Although, I will not be detailing how to build a journey map for every section of the Customer Life Cycle, I will take you through one example to show you how you create a journey map.

EXAMPLE OF BUILDING A JOURNEY MAP FOR THE IMPLEMENTATION SECTION OF A CUSTOMER LIFE CYCLE MODEL

If the CX Implementation were working on the journey map for their Implement section of their Customer Life Cycle model, we would have the team start with the question "We just closed a new contract, what is the next step for the customer?". This should be a transition process from sales to services to start the Implement section of the Customer Life Cycle.

Again, the first step is to schedule a journey mapping session with folks from each of the departments that have a primary and/or supporting role during the implementation cycle. These sessions are usually scheduled for half day to full day sessions depending on the size of your target market, the complexity of the implementations required to meet the various types of customers within the target market.

The teams should come armed with their customer and target market research on what potential customers expect as value from your type of solution as well as what has made customers the most successful and contains information from customers who are 2 year or longer veterans with your solution. The teams will want to be able to articulate to the group what they know customers expect and desire as an ROI and real value from your solution as transformational or game changing to their operations or ability to drive growth and results for their company. If the team has the information on what has created this type of ROI and value with your long term customers (customers who have renewed for more than 2 years, preferably 3-4 year customers), this would be ideal.

The team will usually begin with the mapping on one wall what the customer journey is today. You begin with the first step a customer experiences from the close of the deal. Once you define the first step of the process for the Implement section, you will continue with each logical step including workflows that consider different pathways depending on the type of customer, type of solution, etc. The team should then define all processes along the Implementation methodology by each stage of your methodology if you have a methodology in place today. Define the desired outcomes and deliverables that are critical to getting the customer to the customer success criteria that you drives the way you implement today using the 80/20 rule (the majority of your customers). You should consider all departments in the company that would interact with the customer during any of these details processes. Map this workflow from start to finish on one wall or board. The ending of the implementation section is usually at the launch of the solution or go-live or whatever the customer considers "in production" use of your solution.

Once you have documented what your company delivers today as the customer experience for the implement section, you will then move to the other wall or board and begin to design what the visionary customer journey map should be. This is where you will utilize the customer and market research you have gathered, analyzed and made some conclusions on with what has created the most entrenched and loyal customers to date as well as what the potential customers in the market have shared with you as to what they are looking for, what they expect to get from the solution including ROIs in order to make the appropriate spends to purchase your solution. Meaning; is what you offer provide a cost benefit that they can justify as an overall company improvement long term. This is the vision and insight you want to bring to the journey mapping session to debate and design what your visionary customer journey map should look like in order to deliver consistent results for 10 out 10 customers with quality and excellence in service delivery.

It's essential that your implementation team keeps the customer perspective in mind. As you define the details from the customer's perspective, take a walk in their shoes. Play the role of the customer as you ask the question "What next?, What happens now? What do I do next". Determine whether the processes and interactions enhance the customer's experience, improve their knowledge, make it clear as to what the next steps are for their team, and so on. The team will go through the a similar journey map to what happens today, as their may be some very good things already in place that provide benefits to the customer. Be careful, not to throw the baby out with the bath water when coming up with the best visionary state for the new customer journey.

Start mapping out all the steps the team believes will create the right customer experiences along the required steps or stages of your implementation methodology. Include meetings (onsite and calls), planning and design sessions with consulting, requirements definition, building a solution for unit testing and validation, test planning and execution, education programs for the customer team by role, support programs, the transition to customer success, etc.

Once you have the processes defined along with what procedures or policies may be required to support the processes; you will want to go back through and review what roles should be the responsible roles and supporting roles. It is recommended that you designate a "Key Role" or "Quarterback" for each life cycle section. This allows the customer to deal with one person as they are working through the various sections of the life cycle and will give them a sense of someone responsible for their success.

Discuss the goals, objectives, and outcomes for each step. There are company goals you want to achieve at the end of the process; however, make sure you consider how best to accomplish those by delivering a customer experience that encourages the customer to want to interact with your company further. You want your company to be easy to do business with and one that cares about your customers' success.

For example, If you have a methodology with the typical stages of Plan, Design, Build, Test and Deploy; you define the processes and tasks for each stage of the methodology that the consultant would guide the customer through. You would include when and how the customer would go through an education program, interact with the product team and/or utilize their support program. You would also define the deliverables at each stage, the people involved, their responsibilities and authority levels. You would then define the goals and metrics the team will use to monitor the success of the execution of these processes and the customer's perception of how well you execute and delivered on the expectations you set for success and value. You would finish by defining the hand off processes between Sales and Services to start the implementation section and the transition from Services to Customer Success at the end of implementation.

If your business model targets multiple market segments, you'll need to consider the following:

- If the definition of success that produces real value and ROI for each market segment (i.e., enterprise vs. corporate; retail vs. manufacturing; or marketing vs. Information Technology) is significantly different or takes a unique product, service and/or approach?
- Map each of these market segments separately defining the unique success criteria and processes the customer would experience for that market segment.
  - ◊ *Note: Some elements of the process may be the same, but many may have to be different to ensure you meet the goals/metrics that were defined for that section around revenue $, % services $ to license $, time to value, customer satisfaction, growth rates, etc.*

In these sessions of brainstorming with the CX Team, you'll find some very passionate discussions taking place. I would encourage you to let some of these emotions rise to the surface. They'll uncover some of the real customer challenges and concerns your company may be facing. The key to these sessions is for everyone to be open-minded. It is good for the team to hear everyone's thoughts and suggestions. Much of the content from these sessions may not contribute to the final outcome, but the leaders within the team will be able to glean some meaningful and actionable content. I would encourage you to invite a few team members that work on the front lines that talk with customers everyday. Especially ones that work with the expert users of the solution and/or key champions and players that can articulate where the gaps are the customers are finding between expected value and realized value to date.

The following are some of the best questions to ask when you're exploring these ideas and challenges coming from the various CX team members:

- What does this market segment require as a definition of real value that is sticky and/or an ROI to the customer's company or organization?
- Be mindful of defining a delivered solution that makes it easy for your internal team to deliver versus what is required for the customer to find success with real value, which may be more difficult to deliver?
- What will it take to deliver a higher quality of product or service with consistency?
- Will it improve the customer's perception of our company?
- Will it make it easier to do business with you?
- Will your processes help the customer utilize the product or service in the best way possible?

- Does it create clarity for the customer about the company, products or services and how to get the highest value?
- Does it create an opportunity for the customer to consider an expansion or additional products or services?
- Do the outcomes and deliverables produce a transformational effect for the customer?

During these meetings, keep the vision statement the team created during the Vision stage visible to all in the meeting, either by writing it up on the whiteboard, putting up a poster or projecting a slide on a screen. This is the definition of what a successful customer looks like for the market segment you are mapping out. Also outline the key metrics you're trying to improve in order to deliver results to the company that you defined for this section. Those metrics along with the vision for the customer's perception and expectation of success will help guide the team toward your North Star: The vision is what you expect to achieve when all is in place to create a consistent customer for life.

You will document eight elements that make up a single journey map. These are required to define the support system behind the standards, processes, policies and procedures within each section:

- Problems or Challenges the Customer seeks a solution to solve
- The Customer Success Criteria and Expected Outcomes
- The Customer personas at each stage of process
- The workflow defining the processes including decision points
- The internal people with authority and ownership
- The internal team member's roles and responsibilities
- The metrics with targets or goals
- Standards, policies and detailed procedures that need to be documented.

These journey maps have generated the most popular feedback from my customers. That's not just because they were a nice format for viewing the entire vision for a particular section. But, the journey maps also offer a clear and concise way for all the teams across the organizations to discuss:

- How they should communicate with their customers
- How they should service their customers with a clear vision
- How to work collaboratively on a common set of goals
- How to monitor and measure how they are doing using metrics and customer feedback

As the teams evolve over time, they will update the journey maps to reflect the changes necessary to improve their internal processes and work flows including changes to responsibilities, metrics and goals. The journey maps are commonly used to present to the executive team and other organizations to evangelize the Customer Life Cycle model and execution plan for each quarter. It is a nice way to show the new vision for a market segment and discuss some of the organizational and process changes that will generate new standards, policies and procedures on how the company will operate going forward to create consistent customer success and thus, improve company results. The teams can use the journey maps to monitor and discuss how they will continue to improve how customers benefit from their products and ultimately to become indispensable to their customers.

The next figure is an example of a customer experience journey map vision for the Implement section from the Customer Life Cycle Model sample, as shown on page 42:

Figure 9. Customer Experience Journey Map: Implement Stage of the Life Cycle Model

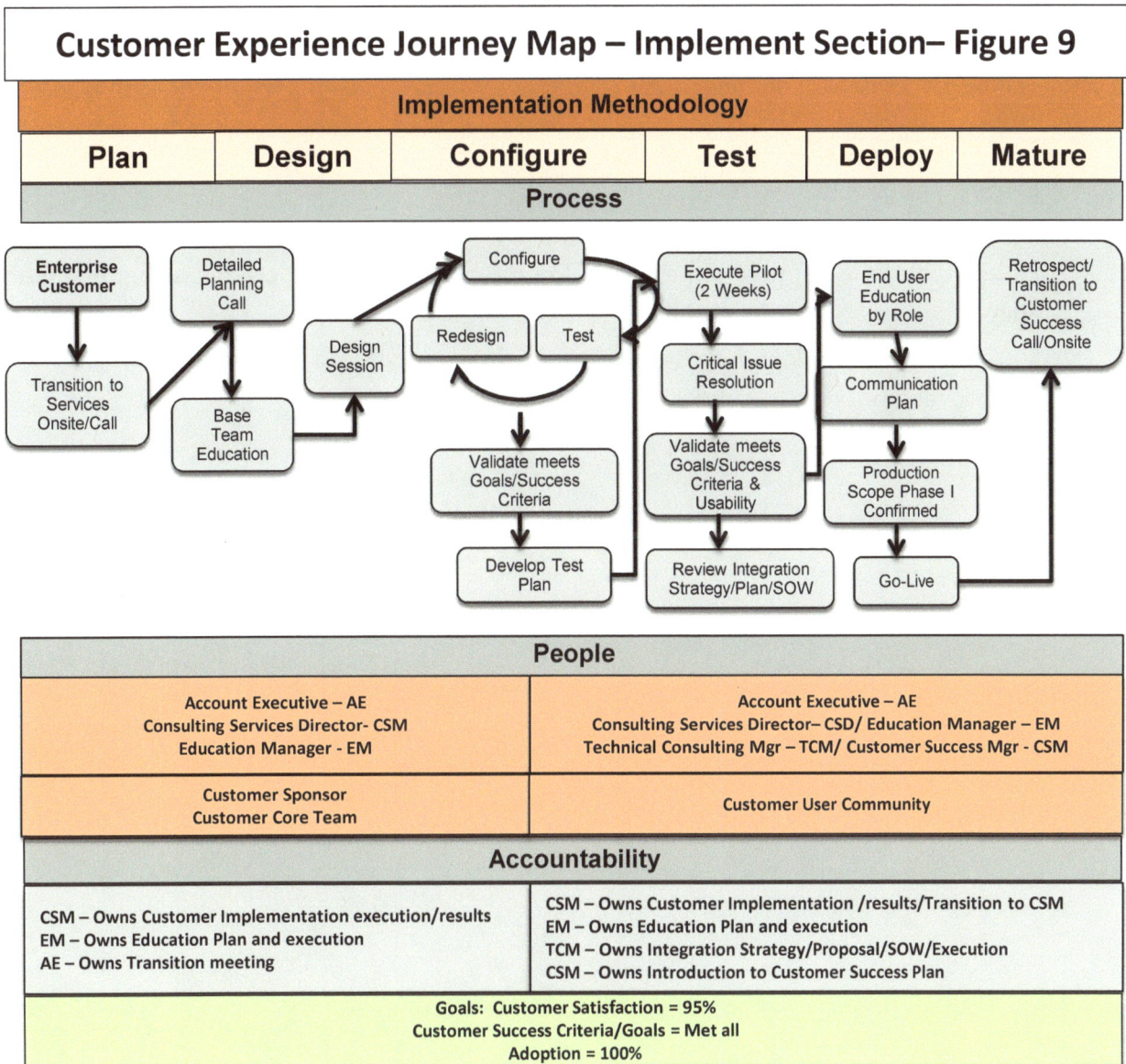

Customer Experience Journey Map – Implement Section– Figure 9

Implementation Methodology

Plan	Design	Configure	Test	Deploy	Mature

Process

- Enterprise Customer
- Detailed Planning Call
- Configure
- Execute Pilot (2 Weeks)
- End User Education by Role
- Retrospect/ Transition to Customer Success Call/Onsite
- Transition to Services Onsite/Call
- Design Session
- Redesign
- Test
- Critical Issue Resolution
- Communication Plan
- Base Team Education
- Validate meets Goals/Success Criteria
- Validate meets Goals/Success Criteria & Usability
- Production Scope Phase I Confirmed
- Develop Test Plan
- Review Integration Strategy/Plan/SOW
- Go-Live

People

Account Executive – AE Consulting Services Director- CSM Education Manager - EM	Account Executive – AE Consulting Services Director– CSD/ Education Manager – EM Technical Consulting Mgr – TCM/ Customer Success Mgr - CSM
Customer Sponsor Customer Core Team	Customer User Community

Accountability

CSM – Owns Customer Implementation execution/results EM – Owns Education Plan and execution AE – Owns Transition meeting	CSM – Owns Customer Implementation /results/Transition to CSM EM – Owns Education Plan and execution TCM – Owns Integration Strategy/Proposal/SOW/Execution CSM – Owns Introduction to Customer Success Plan

Goals: Customer Satisfaction = 95%
Customer Success Criteria/Goals = Met all
Adoption = 100%

A map for the current customer journey map would be the same format as above. The idea is that the team would have this type of format on each whiteboard. One whiteboard would represent the current customer journey map; the other would represent the vision customer journey map. With the future and past presented, the team must analyze each map and document the gaps.

C. Identifying the gaps

The team will now document using a color-coded technique to identify the differences between the Visionary Customer Journey Map and the Current Customer Journey Map.

Using Figure 8, you can create an organized model that shows the gaps or areas of improvement based on color-coding. For example, you can create a color for each of the following within the process section:

- New processes (Red)
- Existing processes that work (Green)
- Existing processes that need improvement (Gold)
- Existing processes that need to be deleted (on the current map, you can put an X through the box)
- You can also color-code each section to separate the identification of the stage, the process, roles required, authority levels, metrics, etc.

Figure 10. Color-Coding of the Visionary Process Showing Gaps

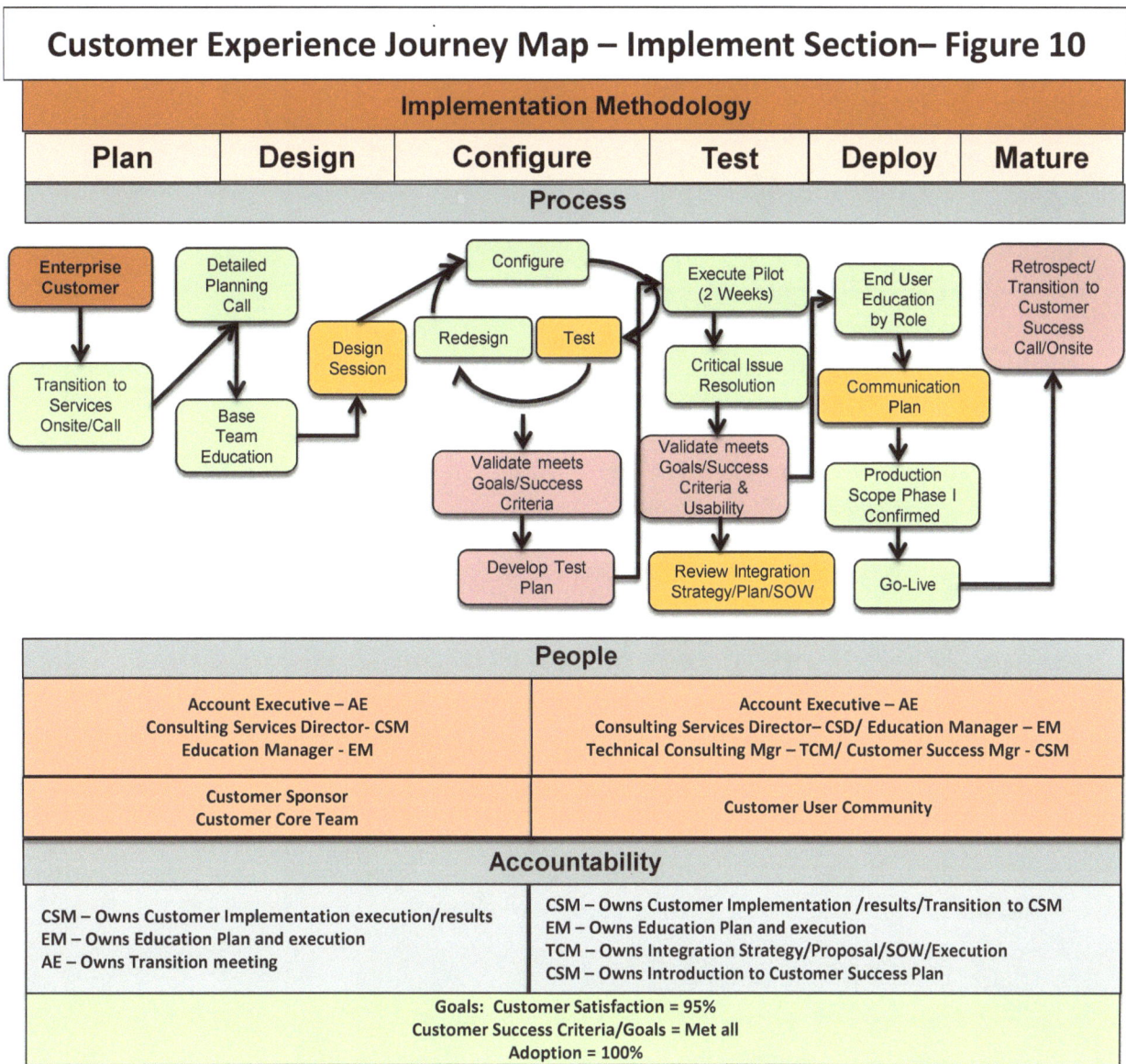

Customer Experience Journey Map – Implement Section– Figure 10

Implementation Methodology

Plan	Design	Configure	Test	Deploy	Mature

Process

Enterprise Customer → Transition to Services Onsite/Call → Detailed Planning Call → Base Team Education

Design Session → Configure ⇄ Redesign → Test → Validate meets Goals/Success Criteria → Develop Test Plan

Execute Pilot (2 Weeks) → Critical Issue Resolution → Validate meets Goals/Success Criteria & Usability → Review Integration Strategy/Plan/SOW

End User Education by Role → Communication Plan → Production Scope Phase I Confirmed → Go-Live

Retrospect/Transition to Customer Success Call/Onsite

People

Account Executive – AE Consulting Services Director- CSM Education Manager - EM	Account Executive – AE Consulting Services Director– CSD/ Education Manager – EM Technical Consulting Mgr – TCM/ Customer Success Mgr - CSM
Customer Sponsor Customer Core Team	Customer User Community

Accountability

CSM – Owns Customer Implementation execution/results EM – Owns Education Plan and execution AE – Owns Transition meeting	CSM – Owns Customer Implementation /results/Transition to CSM EM – Owns Education Plan and execution TCM – Owns Integration Strategy/Proposal/SOW/Execution CSM – Owns Introduction to Customer Success Plan

Goals: Customer Satisfaction = 95%
Customer Success Criteria/Goals = Met all
Adoption = 100%

Note: Gaps represent areas that need focus for changes to existing processes or developed as a new process or deliverable. These would need to be addressed as part of the execution plan.

The gap analysis will clearly illustrate the things that you must stop doing as well as what you must start doing.

D. Defining the people

Once you have the processes well defined you would then define the roles required to execute each process. These roles will be responsible for taking ownership of the following elements for managing the processes assigned to them:

- Monitor execution quality.
- Review exceptions.
- Monitor customer feedback loops.
- Evaluate on a regular basis what's working and what's not.

The roles should be defined with responsibilities and skill sets required to create quality and excellence for each process within each customer life cycle section.

Using Figure 8, you will be able to define the various groups, roles, and responsibilities required at each step of the process to deliver the customer experience.

During the brainstorming sessions, the team may struggle with this concept at each step of the process for the visionary customer experience journey map. Many groups don't want to be responsible nor be measured, especially if they're not held accountable today to standards for delivery or customer experience metrics. Often the team cannot come to a consensus on the roles and responsibilities and who should own each particular element of the process and where the proper handoffs should be. In those cases, it would be appropriate for an Executive Sponsor to attend the next meeting and listen to the areas of concern. The Executive Sponsors or Customer Experience Leadership Team members who represent the various areas should be able to obtain buy-in and agreement on who should own each area and levels of authority including supporting teams. You'll need to have complete agreement on the following for each step of the process:

- Who owns the deliverables for this process and standards?
- Who owns the metric results?
- Who has authority to make the changes as needed in a timely manner?
- Who will gather the customer feedback and provide monthly and quarterly reporting and analysis on trends in what's working and not working?

You will notice in Figure 8 that there is a section to identify the roles involved at each area of the process and then below, a section that defines the authority and accountability level for each of those defined roles.

Figure 11. Bottom inset from Figure 9

Customer Experience Journey Map – Implement Section– Figure 11

People	
Account Executive – AE Consulting Services Director- CSM Education Manager - EM	Account Executive – AE Consulting Services Director– CSD/ Education Manager – EM Technical Consulting Mgr – TCM/ Customer Success Mgr - CSM
Customer Sponsor Customer Core Team	Customer User Community
Accountability	
CSM – Owns Customer Implementation execution/results EM – Owns Education Plan and execution AE – Owns Transition meeting	CSM – Owns Customer Implementation /results/Transition to CSM EM – Owns Education Plan and execution TCM – Owns Integration Strategy/Proposal/SOW/Execution CSM – Owns Introduction to Customer Success Plan
Goals: Customer Satisfaction = 95% **Customer Success Criteria/Goals = Met all** **Adoption = 100%**	

This is important to establish, because it will drive the proper execution and clarity for the team when implementing new processes and managing change in a production environment. It will become part of the corporate climate changes as the organization evolves in its maturity.

The CX team would develop a Customer Journey Map for each section of the Customer Life Cycle using the process defined in this chapter. There may be different team members required from each of the functional organizations for each of your Journey Map sessions. (i.e. For the Acquire section it would be driven by the sales team with the services and marketing leadership team members supporting, the Implement section would be driven by the services team with the sales, product and customer success team members supporting, etc.)

The end result will be a set of journey maps like the example in Figure 10 that represent each section of the Customer Life Cycle.

E. Setting Up customer feedback loops

The customer journey map should have a feedback loop from either the internal teams and/or from the customer at various points in the processes. The following are recommended for creating the most informative feedback loops:

- Define the points of feedback

- Define the type of feedback that is helpful to understand what is working and not working from the customer's perspective
- Define the teams to evaluate feedback data and make decisions on changes required
- Define the Operations team members to manage the implementation changes.

The hardest area of the model to implement and maintain is the evaluation of internal and customer feedback. Remember that the goal of a customer experience model is to drive continuous improvement in the customer's experience with your company, its products, and services in order to create loyalty. So if you simply implement all the changes and then sit back, you'll experience positive results in the beginning that taper off over time.

This methodology is designed as an iterative life cycle that continues as long as you are in business. It is best to track what enables you to achieve the goals for your Customer Life Cycle as well as what detracts from achieving those goals. In order to do this, you will want to create metrics for measuring, monitoring, and evaluating the new processes, programs, offerings, and procedures you put in place as part of the new model. Evaluating the monthly and quarterly trends and results will help drive the decisions on changes and pivots to the strategy and simple management decisions to keep driving towards excellence in your customer's experience.

For example, some of the initial metrics I put in place at WorkFront were a series of internal SLAs for monitoring the first 30 days of a customer's experience.

- The first metric measured the time from the close of the customer transaction to when the customer's planning session was conducted.
- The second metric measured from the customer's planning session to when the customer built a baseline application and the customer's team was actively using the solution or in a pilot phase and beginning to test if the solution was providing real value and ROI.
- The third metric measured from customer's planning session to their confirmed Go-Live date, which we called Customer Time to Value.
- The fourth metric was a customer survey asking for their feedback on the value the solution was providing and if the process and timing met their expectation as well as the quality of services.

These metrics were extremely helpful in understanding where our bottle necks were in moving customers through the implementation lifecycle as well as holding sales accountable for the proper hand offs, debriefs, and introductions to the customer team. They also measured time to value for our customers and provided valuable customer feedback. We measured these by market segment so we could get a feel for the 80/20 rule on the standard expectations we should set for new customers on implementation deliverables, timelines and commitment levels. The focus for these metrics was to ensure the first 30 days of the customer experience was at the highest levels of quality and excellence to set them up for success long term. We added customer feedback metrics at the close of the sale and at their Go-Live to get their perception of their experience with our team and the value they were realizing with our product after the first 30 days in production.

Table 2. Example Metrics Used to track how the Implement section is working in the Customer Life Cycle:

Internal SLAs:
Sales-to-service transition: A welcome call conducted within three days of contract close
Kick-off meeting within seven days of contract close
Customer has had planning call to confirm plan within 7 business days of close
Customer is scheduled for initial education plan within 10 business days of close
Customer Engagement Confirmation for consulting is confirmed by Customer within 10 business days of close
Initial implementation within 60 days of contract close

Customer Experience Goals:
Customer received a roadmap plan within 10 days of contract close
Initial Implementation Success Criteria has been met within 60 days of close
Education program complete and Customer Satisfaction exceeded expectations and provided solid baseline product and solution knowledge to Customer team
Ratings or review for each course in the Education program is at least 4 out of 5 stars or rated as Good or Excellent

Ratings or reviews of consulting team performance in implementing and mentoring Customer Team to a Production Launch is above 98% satisfaction
Customer Engagement >90%
Customer Indispensability >3
Customer Support feedback is 4 or 5 Stars or > 95% Customer
Customer Value and/or ROI is defined and documented (90% of Customers have a value, ROI% or score)
Satisfaction rating or NPS Score of 8 or greater

These metrics can be collected automatically, using various technologies. There are two types of tracking you'll want to consider establishing:

- Internal tracking using a technology that allows the operations team of the organization to track internal SLAs. A project management or work management online collaborative system works best for tracking processes and customer implementations. It will allow you to calculate time in between dates to understand current performance on SLAs, as well as how long the processes are taking (i.e., average time to implementation production (a metric commonly referred to as Time to Value), SLA performance by process, etc.).
- Customer satisfaction ratings can be gathered for different processes as well. I suggest using various techniques for measuring the customer's perception along key processes. These can be simple ratings (i.e., four out of five stars), short surveys (no more than four questions) or simple Yes/No questions about meeting their expectations. If you're using customer surveys, ask short, specific questions about the particular experience and value.

The CX Leadership Team would review these metrics each week/month/quarter, depending on what is the right timing for each metric. The team would have the operations team collect the actual results for these metrics into a dashboard with the targets next to each metric and the variance to the target for review. A weekly/monthly/quarterly rhythm of meetings will help to review these metrics and make decisions on shift points to the strategy or changes required as necessary to move the results towards the targets.

The following are recommended meeting types for reviews:

- 15-minute online team meetings: Best for piloting new processes or newly implemented changes when the team needs fast feedback to make quick changes that impact monthly and quarterly results.

- 30-minute online team meetings: Best for processes already in place and for conducting a quick overall status and focus on solving top-priority problems.
- 1-hour meetings: Best for executive-level reviews with the team to discuss larger, more complex pivots to the strategy or major changes to the Customer Life Cycle model.

Keep the meetings to a minimum, with clear agendas that allow for maximum results. Using online technologies allows the teams to view required information to make decisions that maintain forward progress. The key to executing effective meetings is to be solution-oriented. Try not to get hung up on discussing the problems for too long. It is best to understand the problems and what is preventing the groups from delivering an optimal Customer Life Cycle experience and results; then spend the majority of the time solving the problem and determining the next steps and changes required to deliver more customer value.

Goals should be assigned to each metric. The team should develop reports that show if, when, and by how much the targets have been missed. If these are new standards, processes or procedures when you have no standard or history to review in order to create a goal, you may have to pick an initial target that allows the team some breathing room for the first quarter or two. Then figure out later what a reasonable standard should be. Remember, you don't want the team to lose their excitement or motivation by putting an unrealistic goal on these metrics. It will just make the team give up in the face of impossible goals. However, you should make the goals challenging. If the team still pushes back on the goal and believes it is set too high as a target, explain that it's a stretch goal and is meant to extend your capabilities to establish a more mature organization that delivers better results for customers. Small steps should still produce results by establishing changes that improve the company's ability to deliver a better customer experience.

Developing customer ratings, adoption, and engagement metrics

Ensure that these are meaningful for the type of service and product delivered that can be tracked as a smart goal. These can become team goals for each quarter and be incorporated into a bonus plan to motivate the teams with the most impact on the results.

The metrics defined for an overall customer rating and adoption metric can be more complicated. There are several aspects to each of these metrics.

- Customer ratings have the following elements:
- Customer's perception of the value the solution has brought to the company
- Customer's experience with how easy it was to get to a desirable usage of your product or service that is making an impact and providing real value

- Customer's experience with how easy it is to do business with the company
- Customer's perception of the people they worked with during their customer experiences
- Customer's perception of the quality of service and knowledge of the people they worked with during their experiences with the product or service they engaged

Customer adoption and engagement metrics include the following elements:

- How many licenses or products or services did they purchase?
- Of those purchased, how many have been used or are actively used today?
- How often are they using the solution?
- Are they using the features and functions for the intended purpose?
- Are they using the elements of the solution that result in the entrenched use of the solution as a vital part of operating within their organization or company?
- Is their usage of the solution growing over time?
- Is their usage of the solution a vital part of doing their day-to-day operations?
- Does the use of the solution make them more effective, more efficient, reduce costs or increase revenues?
- How does your solution make their job, operations or ability to deliver their solution easier, better or more efficient?

Note: These questions help define how indispensable the product is to the organization

One of the most transformational developments we made in the Customer Life Cycle measurements at WorkFront was the development of a predictive model using our customer data on adoption, renewal history, and product usage. We plugged the data collected around our customer's activities and usage of the product into a statistical model and found some interesting predictors of renewals and expansion activities. Armed with this information, we were able to utilize our limited resources more productively in order to provide a higher level of service to the customers that needed it. We were able to divide and conquer thus hitting all of our goals each quarter while growing our accounts with a higher capacity utilization of our team members.

The Customer rating information is usually collected by a services team member or operations team (e.g., customer support, education, consultant or customer success representative). Most companies use a 1–4 metric system to evaluate the answer to each of the questions. The reason for the 4-metric (and not 5) is to force the customer to decide if their perception or experience was good or bad. In a 4-metric system you may use the following type of definitions:

4 – Excellent, above expectations

3 – Good, met expectations

2 – Fair, did not meet all expectations

1 – Bad, did not meet any expectations

If the customer has a number that sits in the middle, it's likely that they will go for the neutral decision, which isn't possible in this 4-metric evaluation. They either had a good experience, a 3 or 4, or a bad experience, a 1 or 2. What I like about this approach is that it allows for teams who are in the beginning stages of their maturity model to allow for a good result to be a 3 (good). A 3 in most cases meets the 80/20 rule as well, meaning that 80% of your customers who experience a 3 will remain customers. Again, the goal is to set reasonable goals for the team to achieve so they feel successful for all the hard work they put into making the right changes. Obviously, if the results are still a 1 or 2, then the team will acknowledge the need for more changes or a pivot on the strategy. The Customer feedback loops will become more mature over time with the use of online technologies that automate the various touch points on a regular cadence to track key points along the Customer Life Cycle. These can change based on performance to ensure you understand how to continue to grow the customer base and expansion opportunities with improved value and ROI.

Obtaining good customer feedback information was a key shift point in optimizing the Customer experience at WorkFront. The Services teams (Consulting, Education, Support, and Customer Success) all had different feedback mechanisms in place that helped the teams to make quicker decisions on changes to our approaches, timeliness, and quality of deliverables throughout the customer's engagement with our teams. However, when we first started asking customers about their experience and perception, the answers weren't very positive. Remember my mantra "*The Customer's Perception is our Reality*". We focused on specific areas where we had many Customers provide similar feedback on challenges in the product and elements of our services. We used this information to engaged with the customers to develop changes to our products and services and had them actively engaged to review the changes and provide further feedback in order to validate their perception of Workfront was confirmed as a long term partner in helping their companies to be more successful.

The good news was that the corrections were all relatively easy to make. As a focused team, we made the changes quickly. In fact, the results of the surveys turned positive by the within a few quarters. Within three quarters we had all service (education, consulting, and support) areas above the 95% customer satisfaction ratings in all the key areas we measured and 98% of our customer interviews had a positive perception of our company and product. The residual effect was the increase in customer expansion opportunities.

Developing a maturity level analysis

Once you've defined your Customer Life Cycle Model with the detailed Journey Maps for each section of your Customer Life Cycle, it's time to assess where each unit or organization is located on the maturity model. Most teams can review a maturity model like the one presented earlier in Figure 1 (and repeated here as Figure 11) and determine intuitively which level their organization is at on the maturity levels.

Figure 2. Customer Experience Maturity Model

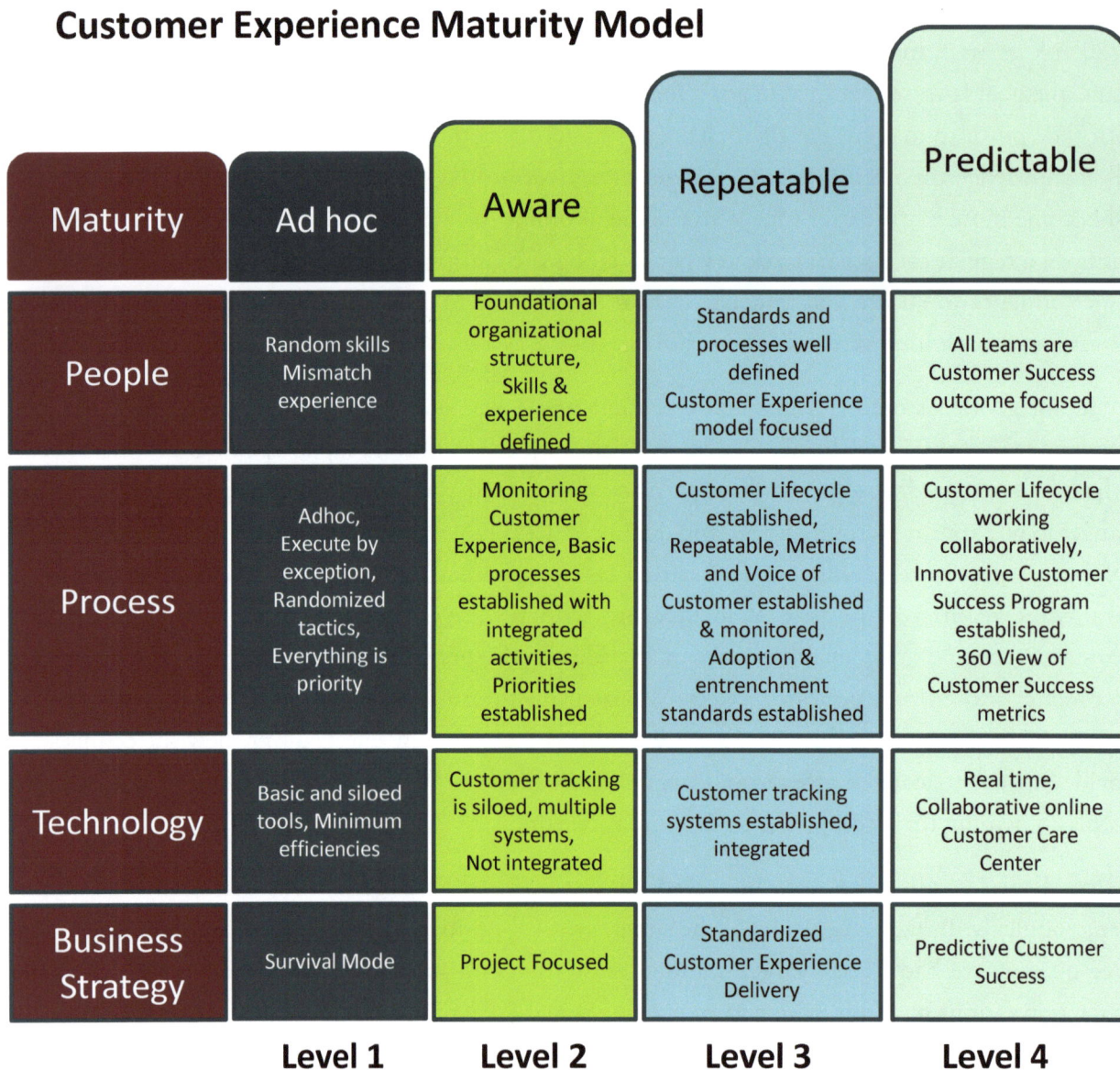

Customer Experience Maturity Model

Maturity	Ad hoc	Aware	Repeatable	Predictable
People	Random skills Mismatch experience	Foundational organizational structure, Skills & experience defined	Standards and processes well defined Customer Experience model focused	All teams are Customer Success outcome focused
Process	Adhoc, Execute by exception, Randomized tactics, Everything is priority	Monitoring Customer Experience, Basic processes established with integrated activities, Priorities established	Customer Lifecycle established, Repeatable, Metrics and Voice of Customer established & monitored, Adoption & entrenchment standards established	Customer Lifecycle working collaboratively, Innovative Customer Success Program established, 360 View of Customer Success metrics
Technology	Basic and siloed tools, Minimum efficiencies	Customer tracking is siloed, multiple systems, Not integrated	Customer tracking systems established, integrated	Real time, Collaborative online Customer Care Center
Business Strategy	Survival Mode	Project Focused	Standardized Customer Experience Delivery	Predictive Customer Success
	Level 1	Level 2	Level 3	Level 4

However, a true assessment reviews every aspect of the customer life cycle and determines the maturity level for each organization that contributes to the execution of each section of the customer life cycle.

For example, in evaluating the design of the Customer Life Cycle, you would review how each of the organizations interact with the customer along the life cycle. Each organization would be assessed to determine its level of maturity. You may discover that the Product organization has already put standards, measurements, and customer service feedback loops and metrics in place for each process they have in place to deliver a quality product consistently and could be at a level 3 in the maturity model. At the same time, the Services organization could be at a level 2 and the Marketing organization could be at a level 1. It is very common for companies to have different departments at different levels of maturity especially for those companies under $100 million in revenue.

Much depends on the company's internal organizations. If these organizations all report up through different executives or leaders, they may all work with different management styles. Some are more sophisticated and experienced than others. The first step is to understand how each organization views the company landscape. Then the team can understand the political obstacles that they will need to overcome in order to get all the organizations functioning at the same maturity level.

The essential reason to understand the maturity level of each organization is to determine the goal for the first phase of implementing the Customer Life Cycle company-wide. The following is an example of simple evaluation of the functional areas of the organization:

Figure 12. Company Maturity Evaluation

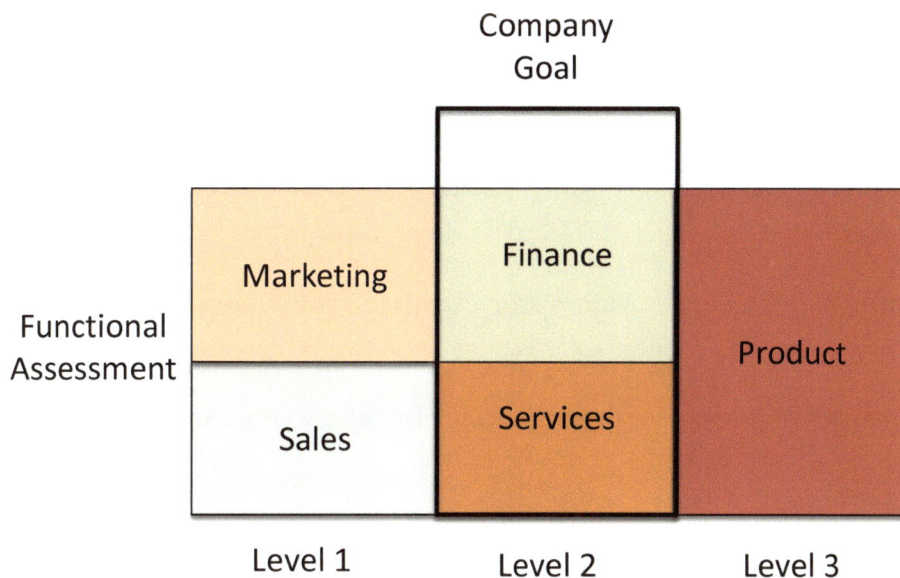

For example, if the Sales organization overall is at a level 2 and the Product organization is at a level 3 and the Marketing and Services organizations are at a level 1, then the first phase goal should be to get all organizations executing at a minimum level 2 in order to create a consistent Customer Life Cycle. From there, the company can improve performance through the maturity stages and optimize the customer experience appropriately within each section of the Customer Life Cycle and as a team. By achieving these goals, the company will avoid having one organization creating an amazing customer experience in a few areas of the Customer Life Cycle, while another organization is still trying to get the foundation in place to create some kind of consistency to their ability to deliver quality and excellence in a timely manner. This is what creates a roller coaster ride in the customer's experience along the Customer Life Cycle. This uneven company performance creates an inconsistent customer experience and risks losing customers. The overall goal of the company is to get all of the departments at a level 2 to start with and then grow and mature through levels 3 and 4 together. By the time they achieve a level 4 maturity, they should be at a high growth rate with predictability to get to a larger company size without disruption in their performance trends and abilities to adapt to market changes and size.

THE ACTION PLAN

Here you will define the details of the plan with task definitions and assignments to the team.

The most successful implementations give authority along with responsibility. Make sure the assignments you make are not only a good match of skills and experience with the ability to execute, but that they provide the authority to make key decisions.

The use of a technology is essential for the team to provide an automated approach to real-time updates, collaboration, ask questions, get information, and share status updates. Such tools are a critical requirement for enabling efficient and effective management of the standards, processes, and procedures you put in place and track the results for all the metrics that get established. It can create automation capabilities and provide more capacity within the team to spend their time in higher value tasks and management duties.

Document the plan so that all team members can review and agree to the plan. It should include timeline and assignments and then be presented to Executive Sponsors to review and approve.

Make sure the goals and objectives for the stage being planned are clear to the Executive Sponsors, as well as the Customer Experience Team.

The key to successfully managing to the plan is to adopt the following policy:

"No excuses, only solutions."

The Executive Sponsors and key leadership team members will want to coach the team to follow this policy for everything related to customer experience. The core concept is that if you are assigned an activity, you have the authority and autonomy to do whatever is required to complete that activity with quality and excellence, on time, and within budget. In order to accomplish this, team members must always be thinking of solutions to every problem or roadblock that presents itself along the way. If they can't see a way to resolve the problem or roadblock, they get help from the team, the Executive Sponsors or leadership team to either resolve or clear a roadblock.

In order to realize success, you'll want to encourage team members to attend the weekly or daily status meetings with an update to their plan, a list of roadblocks or questions they need help with or decisions. You want the team members discussing what they've accomplished, the possible issues they are facing, and what they're doing or going to do to get it done. Help the team members feel empowered to raise the flag the minute they're facing problems in order to get the right people involved to achieve a resolution. If they still have roadblocks, they should contact the Customer Experience Leadership Team or Executive Sponsors to get support and clearance to continue making progress toward their deliverables.

If the entire team conducts themselves this way, the implementation plan will succeed at a more rapid pace. And all future phases and iterations will go smoothly. Their behavior will become part of the corporate climate and maturity of the organization to implement new elements and to make changes within the customer life cycle with diligence and perseverance in a timely manner.

SETTING THE TIMELINE

Once you've built the team, have your Executive Sponsors and Customer Experience team in place, have determined the goals, and planned for the first phase of the Customer Life Cycle implementation, you will determine a timeline. The timeline should work from a realistic start date so that Customer Experience Team Members can book time into their weekly calendars to focus on the delivery of their project assignments. Then develop your timeline based on tasks and resources assigned, taking holidays and PTO into consideration. Add some slack time for critical path elements. Make sure you include tasks that can work in parallel to consolidate the timeline.

If you end up with an end date that is unsatisfactory to the Executive Sponsors or the Customer Experience Leadership Team, then review the plan in detail with the Customer Experience Team Members in order to validate that the time assigned to each task is accurate. Questions to ask:

- Are there any opportunities to decrease the allocated times on each task?
- Did you miss any opportunities to have tasks work in parallel to other tasks?
- Is there too much slack time built in?

- Can you utilize other resources to help deliver more activities in parallel?
- Are there opportunities to outsource tasks to get more done quicker?

Once the plan has been refined with the most accurate information and a set of deliverables defined by quarter, then the Team Members will need to schedule a meeting with the Leadership Team and Executive Sponsors. The team should present the best business case for extending the end date for final delivery and get their approval. This plan should be reviewed with the Executive team each month or a few times each quarter to share progress, results, modifications and the updated plan for the rest of the year.

The best way to get team buy in is to evangelize the plan to the CX team and have the CX team present to all leaders across the organizations at a monthly or quarterly executive meeting. The milestone dates are important for the team to understand and agree to for a collaborative team to work together effectively and support the priority of delivering on the changes required to mature the company and its ability to delivery consistent customer success with quality and excellence.

The Communication Plan

If it's important to you, then be certain to make the value of the CX Implementation project vital to everyone who will be affected by the final delivery.

Create a marketing plan for communicating the following about the project:

- What will this deliver to the business?
- Why is this important to the business?
- How will it change the way we do business?
- What is the value to customers?
- How will it impact the department or groups within the organizations that it effects?
- What's in it for the employees affected?
- How will it affect these employees?
- How can they help this project be successful?
- What is the timeline and time commitment from their team members?
- What is expected of them as part of the quarterly delivery plan?

By educating the organizations affected and sharing with them the details of the value of the project, they will be able to internalize the information and begin to support the team in any efforts required. Evangelizing in a fun way is always encouraged, especially if you can find ways to make fun of yourselves and the way you may do things today. Then show the new and improved customer experience. The team could have fun creating a video of typical customer experiences today, with as many fun scenarios as possible that everyone would relate to—and then showing what it will look like in the brave new world and the tremendous impact on the customer's success.

Now that the company supports the work of the CX Team, you should also define a communication plan for the team during the implementation phase. That plan should be part of the new company corporate climate going forward.

This usually includes a daily wrap-up session, a brief 15-minute online chat or call that allows everyone to participate in a quick round robin discussion of critical items. The team members will either report "all is good" or share an issue that needs leadership support or resolution. This daily session can be a place where a team member is encouraged to ask for advice if needed.

The team should have a formal 30-minute status meeting once a week or biweekly, with a set agenda that includes the following elements:

- Introduction of new or changed Team Members
- Summary status of the overall progress of the Customer Life Cycle implementation
- Executive-level communications, which may include an announcement on strategy changes or new strategies that might need to be considered in the current execution plan.
- Round robin by major functional area (sales/services/marketing/product/finance/etc.)
  - What's completed with any highlights they might want to advertise
  - Issues that need the team's support
  - Upcoming changes in the organization that are important for the team to be aware of.
  - Challenges they need a decision on or guidance to move forward
  - Highlight of improvements in key Smart Goals' performance to date (once the initial phase of your customer Life Cycle is underway)

Monthly or quarterly, the team should present to the Executive Sponsors the overall progress of the Customer Life Cycle model delivery. The agenda is a condensed version of the above, which highlights key successes, deliverables, and positive influences on Executive level key metrics.

Now that you have a solid CX Plan and Design that the team has agreed to and communicated out to the company, the CX team is ready to begin developing the new elements and changes identified during the design stage.

CHAPTER 7

CX IMPLEMENTATION METHODOLOGY – DEVELOP STAGE

THE DEVELOP STAGE:

The purpose of the Develop Stage is to develop the detailed elements that each organization defined in the plan and design stages for of all sections of the Customer Life Cycle for a specific target market.

At this point, the CX Team should have designed and documented a journey map for each section of the Customer Life Cycle: Acquire, Implement, Value, and Expand.

For each of these journey maps, the team will have completed a gap analysis that defines the difference between what the company does today and what they planned to do in the visionary journey map designed for each section of the customer life cycle model. This gap analysis will create a list of requirements that would require a plan and design with specific outcomes or changes identified in processes, standard, policies or procedures. These requirements may be developed or evolved from an existing standard, process or procedure or created as new to support the delivery and outcomes defined in the journey map. The CX Team will allocate these tasks to each of the appropriate organizations.

Figure 13. Customer Experience Methodology: Develop Stage

The Customer Experience Methodology – Figure 13

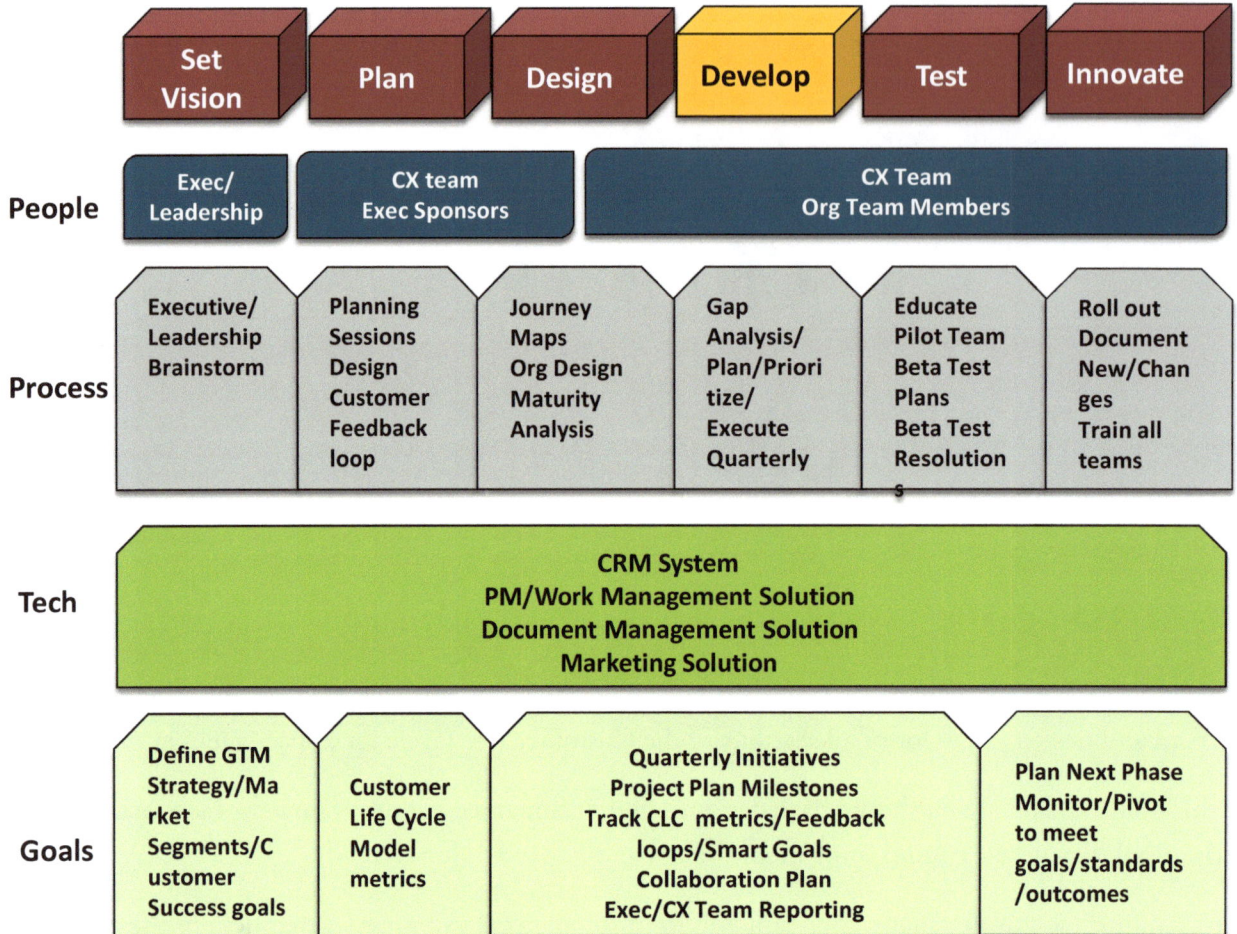

Set Vision	Plan	Design	Develop	Test	Innovate

People				
Exec/ Leadership	CX team Exec Sponsors	CX Team Org Team Members	

Process

Executive/ Leadership Brainstorm	Planning Sessions Design Customer Feedback loop	Journey Maps Org Design Maturity Analysis	Gap Analysis/ Plan/Prioritize/ Execute Quarterly	Educate Pilot Team Beta Test Plans Beta Test Resolution	Roll out Document New/Changes Train all teams

Tech

CRM System
PM/Work Management Solution
Document Management Solution
Marketing Solution

Goals

Define GTM Strategy/Market Segments/Customer Success goals	Customer Life Cycle Model metrics	Quarterly Initiatives Project Plan Milestones Track CLC metrics/Feedback loops/Smart Goals Collaboration Plan Exec/CX Team Reporting	Plan Next Phase Monitor/Pivot to meet goals/standards /outcomes

The following is an example of a gap analysis from the journey maps (today vs. visionary). This will become your roadmap for executing the delivery of the elements in a phased approach that will lead to an execution plan that delivers on the new visionary Customer Life Cycle:

Figure 14. Gap Analysis

Plan Customer Life Cycle Implementation Summary Action Plan (Based on Gap Analysis)		
	Q1	**Q2**
Acquire	Incorporate Scoping Session into Sales Methodology standards for Market Segment	Create Transition Process from Sales to Services
	Create Marketing Materials for Internal/External messaging around Customer Life Cycle	Develop new SOWs and SKUs for New Services Programs
	Create New Program offerings with Product and Services Program	Create Value Selling Workshop for Sales team
	Create Education/Marketing Workshop to communicate Customer Life Cycle Model to Company	Execute Workshops on new Customer Life Cycle Model
	Create New Program offerings with Product and Services Program	Pilot Selling new Solution Programs
Implement	Define Customer Success that deliver Prescriptive Outcomes with values (programatize offerings)	Develop Customer Life Cycle Model Metrics Dashboard
	Develop New Services Methodology	Create New Maturity Model for Market Segment
	Develop New Templates for All Supporting Document Deliverables for each stage of the New Methodology	Create a Education Program to deliver knowledge transfer to meet Customer Success definition
	Develop Services profitability model	Create Baseline Implementation Definition
Value	Create Process for Consultant to transition account to Customer Success	Determine system for tracking Customer Success by customer & action items
	Create Customer Success program by Market Segment	Define Customer Dashboard and key metrics
	Create a model for CS team to utilize key services resources for solving customer problems	Educate Serevices team on new programs and offerings to support expansion opportunities
	Create processes for CS to incorporate required resources to resolve customer issues (using Cons/Edu/Support/Product teams) as needed	Create process for transition Customers from Services to Sales for processing expansion opportunities back through the Sales Cycle methodology
Expand/ Renew	Create process for AE to be supported by CS and Services to support Expansion opportunity closure	Create Process for Partnering Services & Sales to ensure renewals and expansions are cohesive and easy for customer to activate

The gap analysis lays out quarter by quarter the top-priority items to be developed or modified within each life cycle section. The team can develop a gap analysis using a scrum methodology. They can write each of the identified changes (gaps) on sticky notes and affix them on a wall or whiteboard under each stage name in order of what is most important. There are some items that must be done before other items can be done; in these cases, they are usually addressed in one calendar quarter and the next item is addressed in the subsequent quarter. If there are items that can be accomplished quickly, you can do them in the same quarter. Once you have all of your gap items identified for each stage in a prioritized order, the team will assess the approximate time for completion and assign them to the right calendar quarters and responsible team member. For example, if you are currently in Q4, then you would start your plan to begin the development cycle for these items in Q1. Now that you have a scrum wall that has laid out all gap items by section by quarter, you can create your implementation project plan that defines all the tasks, assignments and milestone due dates for the requirements of the Customer Life Cycle.

The project plan will detail all tasks for changes and development requirements identified in the gap analysis. I recommend that you define the Customer Life Cycle section and all the tasks required to implement the elements of the journey map for this section of the life cycle. This means that the gap analysis might have identified 20-plus elements that you need to address. However, if the Phase I CX Implementation plan is to improve from a maturity Level 1 to a 2, you'll only put on the development list those items that support these stages of maturity progression. You'll add the rest of the items in the follow-on phases of your Customer Experience implementation plan. They could all be done in Phase II or might have to be split into a Phase II, Phase III, etc. Remember, one phase of a Customer Experience implementation plan could be 60 to 90 days. So with a focused team supported by Executive Sponsors, you can take your company from a customer experience maturity Level 1 to a 3 within a year. This helps you plan all the changes required to ensure the realization of each of your visionary journey maps over time with a phased approach.

In the Develop phase, the team should have a plan for the detailed list of elements being changed or developed as new elements for the quarter. Each quarter the team should have assignments for delivering these elements within or by the end of the quarter.

The Plan may be updated at the end of the Develop stage based on a better understanding of what it will take to build, develop, test and roll out all the elements defined in the Gap Analysis.

If an element requires a true test period or formal pilot, then the team will develop all the content, processes, procedures, etc. in the current quarter and have it ready to pilot in the next quarter. This would include making sure the team allows enough time to educate the pilot team prior to the start of the pilot testing. If the element only requires a short period of time to develop and put in place for use in daily operations and execution, then no formal testing or pilot may be needed. In this case, the element can go straight to educate, document, communicate, and then launch.

CHAPTER 8

CX IMPLEMENTATION METHODOLOGY – TEST STAGE

The Test Stage

The purpose of the Test stage is to test the new changes and elements to ensure they work properly and they deliver the expected level of customer experience. This is the correct stage to make changes and ensure they will create the impact that is expected. Once they are ready to roll out for the day-to-day delivery or operations of the business, then you will need to educate the appropriate team members internally. Some elements will only require an internal education program. But some will also require notification and education for the customer prior to rolling to production use or day-to-day operations.

At this point, you will have developed the required elements, made changes to existing elements, and created some new processes, standards, procedures, offerings or content that you are ready to implement. However, you must test these new elements and changes in order to verify they will deliver the type of customer experience that you have designed. Therefore, you need to plan for testing the new offerings, content, processes, procedures, and policies that you have developed. Once they have been tested in a small pilot with a few team members and a select few customers for feedback, you can then determine the appropriate date for making the changes effective or for launching new elements. Then you need to plan an education program for rolling out internally and for announcing and notifying customers, if it's appropriate.

Figure 15. Customer Experience Methodology: Test Phase

The Customer Experience Methodology – Figure 15

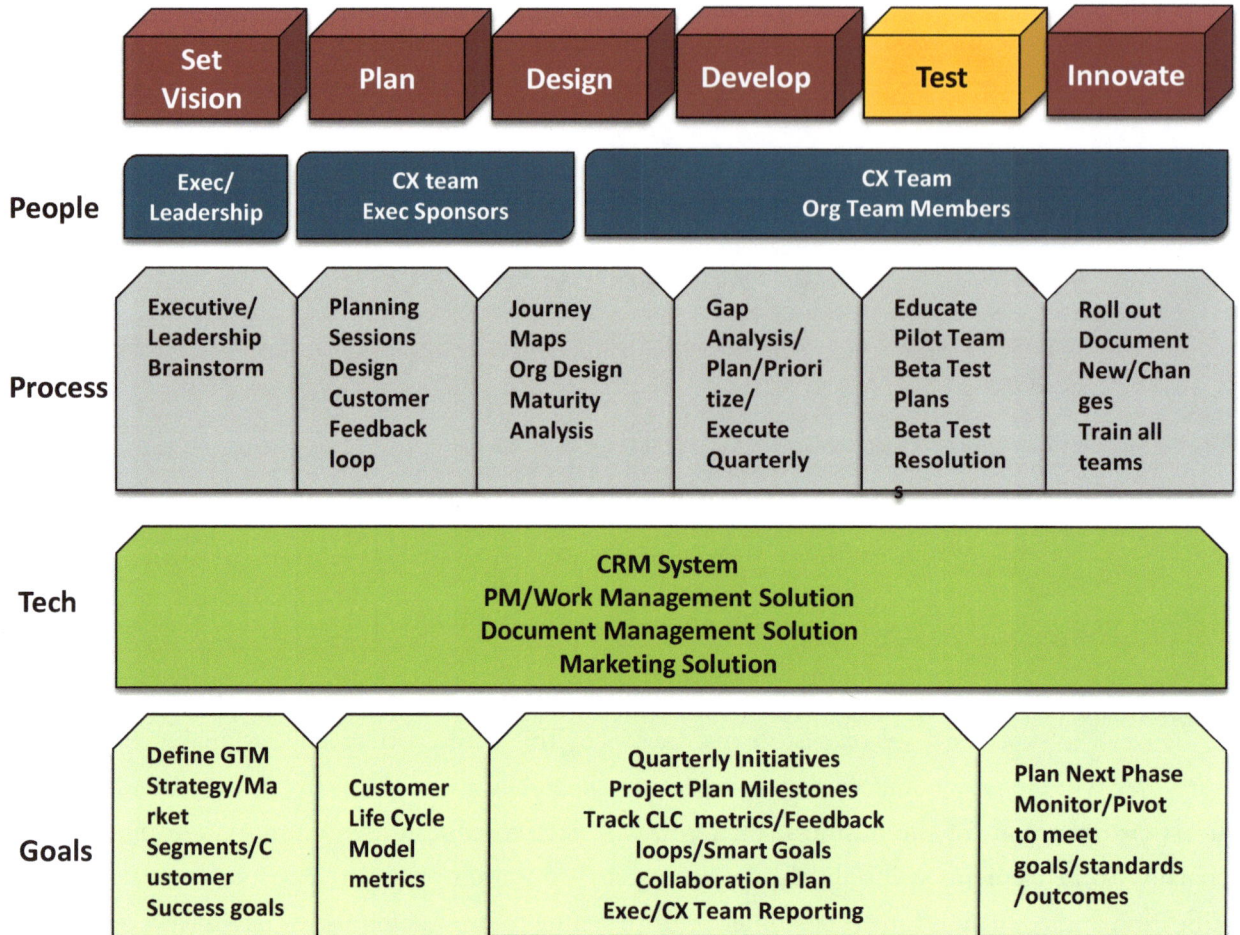

Set Vision	Plan	Design	Develop	Test	Innovate

People	Exec/ Leadership	CX team Exec Sponsors	CX Team Org Team Members			

Process	Executive/ Leadership Brainstorm	Planning Sessions Design Customer Feedback loop	Journey Maps Org Design Maturity Analysis	Gap Analysis/ Plan/Priori tize/ Execute Quarterly s	Educate Pilot Team Beta Test Plans Beta Test Resolution	Roll out Document New/Chan ges Train all teams

Tech	CRM System PM/Work Management Solution Document Management Solution Marketing Solution

Goals	Define GTM Strategy/Ma rket Segments/C ustomer Success goals	Customer Life Cycle Model metrics	Quarterly Initiatives Project Plan Milestones Track CLC metrics/Feedback loops/Smart Goals Collaboration Plan Exec/CX Team Reporting	Plan Next Phase Monitor/Pivot to meet goals/standards /outcomes

The Test Plan

Several levels of testing are recommended for each element, whether it is a new offering, content, policy, process or procedure,—or a slight change to one of these elements.

A Simple Test Plan: For a simple change or new element being implemented, you would create a test plan that documents the process in the appropriate reference guide. These guides can include playbooks, operational reference guides, etc. Determine the date the new or changed process will take effect. Have a few Team Members review the details and provide feedback to ensure that it will deliver the expected results and experience to the customer.

A Complex Test Plan: For a more complex change or new element being implemented, you would also create a test plan that documents the element in the appropriate reference guide. These guides can include playbooks, operational reference guides, etc. Determine the date that the new or changed process will take effect. In addition, you should create a test team to test the element in a pilot program from two weeks to 90 days, depending on the element. For processes, procedures or policy changes, a few weeks of testing with live prospects or customers usually suffices. For new products or offerings, I recommend a 60- to 90-day testing period including customer feedback and a few iterative changes to validate the impact is an improvement.

Let's use the example of a new product offering requirement defined in the Acquisition journey map to meet the requirements of a Mid-market target market segment. The CX Team would use the following process to plan and execute a proper test plan for testing the new product offering:

- Meet with the Sales team to walk through the target market customer personas and agree on the success criteria and ROI the new product or service offering would be expected to deliver
- Work with marketing to develop, design and test the new marketing documents that defines the new product offering, value, what's included, implementation plan, and price; as appropriate.
- Develop and test the new pricing policy and prospect qualification requirements.
- Identify the Mid-market sales team members who will pilot selling the new offering in the next quarter.
- Educate the pilot sales team on the new process, qualifications, and policies around the new offering and provide the reference documentation. Usually this would be put into their CRM (e.g., Salesforce, etc.) library of documents.
- Identify and train the services team members required to support the test cycle process.
- Determine a pilot start date. If the current quarter is Q4, the pilot would start in Q1.
- Create a customer and internal feedback loop process using technology to automate feedback and enable quick issue resolution during the pilot.
- At the 30-day mark, evaluate feedback and make any changes for the second half of the pilot.
- At the 60-day mark, complete the pilot and evaluate all feedback and customer perceptions of sales cycle experience and value. Feel free to use any customer feedback techniques including a questionnaire being sent to the customers that purchased the new offering and asking for feedback using a short, four-question survey, interviews, NPS scoring, etc.

- Meet with the CX team to discuss results of the pilot test. Confirm agreement on final offerings, pricing, marketing approach and effective date of the launch.
- Make all final changes (process, standards, outcomes, pricing, sales and marketing materials, etc.) to create a production ready offering.

Test Results Evaluation

The pilot team will want to provide feedback within a set period of time that is based on the pilot cycle time. For example, if the plan includes a two-week pilot, then the feedback would be evaluated at the end of each week. If changes are required, then a retest may be required in order to ensure the results meet expectations for the new offering, element or change.

The CX team would present the results from the Pilot test to the leadership team to evaluate if the new offering, element or change produced the improvements expected and if the investment is worth pursuing as a standard. The goal is to improve the customer experience and to drive the company results in the right direction. If the change didn't produce the expected outcomes and improvements, then it may not be an appropriate change in the current environment. The risk of pursuing changes that don't produce improvements or desired results is that they can be come a distraction and derail resources and budget unnecessarily. The CX team can be given the authority to decide to maintain the current state or to determine that the change is the right decision and recommend the timing for rolling it out as a new company wide standard, but many companies require an executive level review and approval for some changes.

The test phase is an important step in the implementation process for ensuring that the changes or new elements meet the requirements and expected results for improving the customer experience within the life cycle section that will deliver better results for the customer.

Once the test results have been accepted, the team is ready to develop the education plan to ready the teams for the roll out.

The Education Plan

In the education plan, the CX team can utilize their current education department or team if they have one in place; otherwise, they will need to formulate a process for educating the team members who will have an impact to their current standards, policies, processes and/or procedures. These are team members across various functional areas. For example, in the Customer Life Cycle, the figure shown again here from an earlier chapter, if the change is a new offering or process identified within the Acquisition section, then there may be team members from the other functional areas (i.e. Services, Marketing, Finance or Product) that may need to be included in the education plan.

Figure 6. Customer Life Cycle Model

The Customer Experience Methodology — Figure 6 Customer Lifecycle Model

If we look at the Implement section, the supporting roles are usually Education, Product, Customer Success, Support, and Marketing. You may need to include many of these team members in the education plan to ensure quality and consistent execution of the changes and a smooth customer experience process.

The CX team will need to evaluate how many sections are affected by the change and who is involved in the workflow points along the Customer Life Cycle for the change or new program being implemented. The team would review the roles required to support the change or who would be effected by the change and include them in the education plan.

There are various ways to educate your internal and external teams to prepare them for the changes and new elements. Each type of element may require any one of the following kinds of education approaches:

Table 3. Education Approaches

Education Approach	Description
Notification	An online collaborative notification system in which a select distribution group can be created and notified of a new or changed process, procedure, policy or offering. This can also be a simple email.
Update or New Reference Guide	These can be playbooks, policy and procedure documents or operational guides. They can be stored on shared/collaborative technologies and notifications can be sent to authorized document users.
eLearning	A Learning Management solution that has a library of various education videos, Learning paths defined, presentation decks that are self-paced learning reference materials. They can be used for internal or external educational programs.
Workshop/Classroom Training	Instructor-led in-person educational course offerings with materials to support the training of any new or changed standard, process, procedure, policy, or offering. Workshops are usually short training sessions of 30 minutes to two hours. They can be conducted using online technologies to present the training materials and allow for interactive discussions and questions. Classroom training is more formal and usually involves one or more days of training to educate the team on various topics. In both cases, they can be video-recorded and put up on the library to allow for self-paced training. This works well for global rollouts to accommodate different time zones.
Capstone	Some educational sessions are best served by having a capstone course with a presentation, exercises and/or project required. These can also be self-recorded videos showing a presentation of the materials that is submitted for validation. Capstones can hold the team accountable for learning the required material in a specific timeframe and a more thorough manner.

For example, at WorkFront, we rolled out two new service programs to improve the results in two of our target market segments; one to support the Enterprise Market segment and the other to support the Mid-Market segment. Because these were new programs that utilized a new sales approach, implementation methodology and customer success program, we created an education workshop that we rolled out to all organizations. We videotaped the sessions and allowed the functional leaders to hold the Pilot team members accountable for completing the education course. Our Education team put these into our Learning Management System (LMS) as part of our internal learning path options for employee training. The organizations used the LMS as a way to get all team members trained and ready to Pilot and support the new changes. The workshop included changes to messaging, value propositions, success criteria and/or ROIs, and marketing materials. The sessions walked through the changes to processes, policies and procedures to get everyone on the Pilot team aligned.

We planned our pilot program, where one focused sales team in each market sold and executed the new program with the services team for one quarter. We monitored feedback both internally and externally (from the customer). We then made changes necessary to ensure the programs were more consumable and produced outcomes that made a significant impact for the customer including becoming more indispensible to their daily operations. We made some internal changes as well in our processes and procedures to make the experience smoother and positive for the customers in each market. We ran the pilot for one quarter, collecting feedback, making a few changes and retesting with a few customers. The results proved that the new programs hit the mark for our customers improving the sales cycle close time, the average sales price and the implementation plan for long term customer success. At the end of the quarter, we reviewed the results with the executive team and provided our recommendation to roll out the new programs effective the next quarter. We then rolled out the programs companywide for all teams in both markets in the following quarter.

The most effective Pilots are the ones where the teams were well educated prior to the start. This allows them to run the Pilot in full production mode, which provides more accurate customer feedback. It leads to better decision making on how to design, develop and rollout changes within your Customer Life Cycle in alignment with your go to market strategy on a continuous basis. It also provides the education team with the proper lead time to create high quality education content and test various distribution vehicles prior to the full roll out for new programs and products.

The education plan should be scheduled within a few weeks from launching a pilot test phase or from launching a change into production. The following is an example of an education plan:

Figure 16: Example Education Plan

Education Plan – Figure 16

Role	Courses	Milestone	Venue
Sales Team	Sales Methodology Workshop Services Methodology Selling a Roadmap to Success Sell the Right fit Services Program	Q1	Virtual/Onsite
Services Team (Education/ Consulting/ Support)	Services Methodology Certification Selling a Roadmap to Success Services Programs Customer Success Programs and goals	Q1	Virtual/Onsite
Customer Success	Sales Methodology Workshop Services Methodology Certification Selling a Roadmap to Success Recommending the right Services Programs	Q1	Onsite/ELearning
Finance	Services Programs	Q1	Virtual/ELearning
Product	Services Programs	Q1	Onsite

Many of my clients have utilized their internal education teams to support creating the content and conducting the courses or workshops for each educational requirement. If you do not have an internal education team established yet, you will want to engage one or more of the team members that are subject matter experts and/or has experience in creating educational content, conducting education courses and workshops. You can also utilize the marketing teams to help create videos and presentation materials.

Notice that these workshops and trainings are scheduled by quarter, based on when the project plan is scheduled to rollout the new programs and changes. Some workshops and trainings will continue each quarter to support new and transferred employees, promotions or job changes as part of their onboarding program. For example the sales certification and services certification programs should be quarterly offerings at a minimum. We recommend trying to organize new hires and internal changes into classes and then scheduling these certification courses so that you can have people work together in teams and support each other during their onboarding certification program.

After the testing and education programs have been scheduled and executed, the team will need to plan for the production rollout of the new product, services, offerings, policies, standard, processes, and procedures in support of the Customer Life Cycle implementation.

CHAPTER 9

CX IMPLEMENTATION METHODOLOGY –INNOVATE STAGE

The purpose of the Innovate stage is to roll out new elements and changes into the day-to-day operations for the appropriate teams responsible for executing.

This is the point at which the team would plan to rollout the new program, element or change on the scheduled effective date. Now the team can create a readiness plan for executing the new element or change as part of the company's standard operations.

Once the effective date for rolling out the new program or change is confirmed by the team, they need to execute the following production readiness activities within one to two weeks from the effective production date:

Documentation: All new or changed product, services, templates, documents, contracts, offerings, policies, standards, processes, and procedures have been documented and published to their document management system for company wide sharing. A communication or notification would go out to the company employees describing the change, purpose and a link to where the reference documents can be found.

Review and Approval: The Customer Experience Team should determine if a review of the documentation to ensure accuracy and an approval from the appropriate leadership team members is required. If so, the document should go to the appropriate team members for review and approval prior to sending the final gold copy to the appropriate library.

Figure 17. Customer Experience Methodology: Innovate Phase

The Customer Experience Methodology – Figure 17

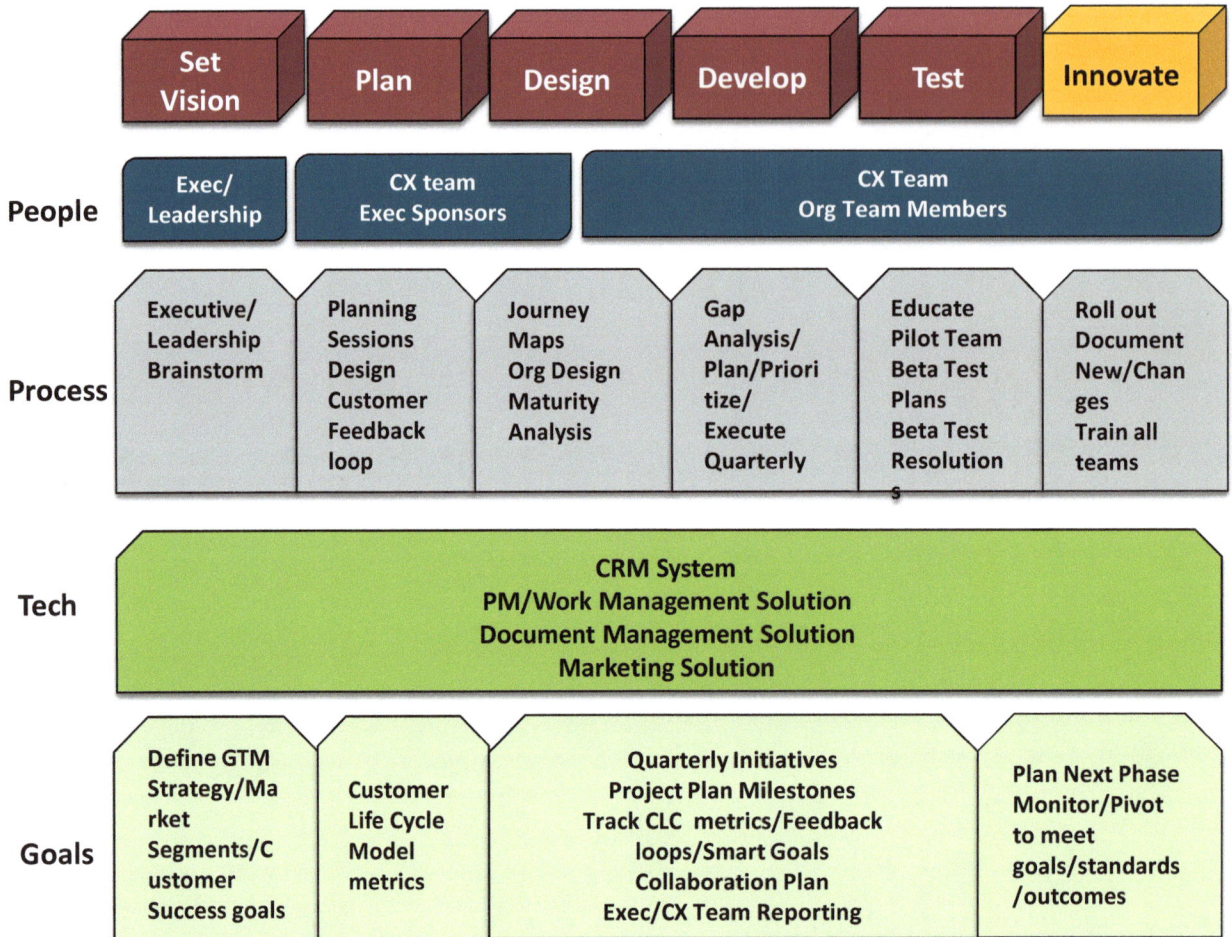

	Set Vision	Plan	Design	Develop	Test	Innovate

People	Exec/ Leadership	CX team Exec Sponsors		CX Team Org Team Members		
Process	Executive/ Leadership Brainstorm	Planning Sessions Design Customer Feedback loop	Journey Maps Org Design Maturity Analysis	Gap Analysis/ Plan/Priori tize/ Execute Quarterly s	Educate Pilot Team Beta Test Plans Beta Test Resolution	Roll out Document New/Chan ges Train all teams
Tech	CRM System PM/Work Management Solution Document Management Solution Marketing Solution					
Goals	Define GTM Strategy/Ma rket Segments/C ustomer Success goals	Customer Life Cycle Model metrics	Quarterly Initiatives Project Plan Milestones Track CLC metrics/Feedback loops/Smart Goals Collaboration Plan Exec/CX Team Reporting			Plan Next Phase Monitor/Pivot to meet goals/standards /outcomes

Change Management process is formalized and documented. A notification has been sent across the company to ensure all employees are notified of the change including how to submit change requests and provide feedback on any areas that are not working well.

Communication Plan: Develop a communication plan and cadence for evaluating what's working and not working in each of the customer life cycle sections and all continuous innovations. Schedule monthly business review meetings with the Customer Experience Team and key Leadership Team members to evaluate the metrics dashboard and performance of key smart goals and results. Schedule weekly business reviews within each organizational leadership team and team members to review Customer performance and feedback.

Analysis and Predictive modeling: Develop a rhythm of reporting trends on key customer metrics along with the collection of customer feedback, thoughts and perceptions of what real value has been realized or not realized. It's always good to asking the Customer what created the most value and ROI for them and why. Develop a predictive model for what elements have the biggest influence on a customer's guarantee of renewal and expansion. There are many data models that utilize customer usage, adoption, length of time as a customer, average contract value and indispensible factors as variables in their statistical modeling. Some companies have develop complex algorithms for using all of these metrics into a scoring system that they test as being close to 100% accurate in predicting churn.

Next Phase Plan: Develop the plan for the next phase of the evolution of the Customer Life Cycle model by creating the plan for the next set of priorities for implementation.

Let's discuss each of the three Production readiness activities in more detail.

Documentation

There are many perspectives on documentation. Too often most documentation is either not utilized as intended or ever read again once it is created. However, my perspective is that most documentation is not user-friendly. It is not created in a short, concise, easily organized, and easy-to-find systems so that the team members can reference the information effectively. We won't discuss best documentation practices here, but we suggest the following key guides to use in support of a typical rollout:

Sales and services playbook. This document would contain these key topics:

- Products
- Services
- Sales, implementation or service approach methodologies
- Pricing and packaged offerings
- Standards and policies
- Discounts and approvals
- Procedures
- Certification requirements
- Partner program
- References

Services Methodology. This document would contain these key topics:

- Methodology Diagram
- Statement of Work document for each program offering
- Customer documentation Templates for each stage of the methodology
- Customer Plan Confirmation Process
- Customer Roadmap by market segment and solution

Customer Experience Guide. This document would contain these key topics:

- Customer Life Cycle Model
- Journey maps for each section
- Key metrics to measure success with current goals
- Customer success program
- Customer Value, Success Criteria and ROIs by target market or market segment

Operational Excellence Guide. This document would focus on how to make it easy to do business with your company and ensure the customer's experience with any organization will be met with quality and excellence. The following are key sections in this document:

- HR Section with all the key topics for employees (employee orientation, equipment, support, PTO, policies, procedures such as time tracking, expense reporting, etc., training, etc.)
- Onboarding process including certifications required.
- Finance section with the key topics for how other organizations interact and collaborate with the Finance team (e.g., sales support, services support, budgeting process, expense reimbursement, customer inquiries, standards, policies, and procedures, etc.)
- IT section with the key topics for how the IT organization supports the rest of the organizations (e.g., equipment, software, service, support, locations, help desk, policies, processes, and procedures to get the support required)
- Marketing section with key topics on how to request marketing support for events and collateral in support of each of the organization's offerings, mostly sales and services, but can be utilized for internal company activities as well. (i.e., processes, policies, and procedures would be included in this section.)
- Product section with key topics around standards and processes for new product releases and updates to existing releases including references to websites and information for the customer to find easy answers.
- Sales section with key topics for getting the sales team involved to help support a customer

and summary information on partner programs and how a company can become a partner.

- Services section with key topics on how to implement and support a customer with the methodology, standards, policies, and procedures for how customers can engage and what standards the company holds themselves accountable to (i.e., customer support service-level agreement goals, product warranties, uptime standards, etc.) The services section generally includes consulting, education, support, and customer success organizations. This would include the details on the online Customer Self Help center to help them obtain quick answers and reference to all key information about your company, products, services, offerings, user groups, knowledge base, etc.

These documents should have various team members assigned to the appropriate sections and held accountable for the accuracy and updates to the information. If a change is required, they should submit the change through the leadership team or Customer Experience Teams as appropriate prior to publishing any update.

If you are using a CRM (e.g., Salesforce, etc.) system with a library, the gold version of these documents can be published in the CRM library or a shared document storage technology that the team members can easily access, no matter where they are located. It's best if these documents can be indexed with search engines that make it easy to find the topics a team member is looking for. Reminders and notifications can be publicized to the entire company when a new version of any of these documents is published and given a reference to the section that has been changed.

REVIEW AND APPROVAL

Each document can go through a review process and approval by members of the Customer Experience Team or the team members responsible for execution of the area of change to ensure accuracy and alignment with the company standards and goals.

Each document will have different team members assigned to each of its sections. These team members will be accountable for updating the sections as changes are processed through the change management process. They will then submit these to the appropriate functional leaders or Customer Experience Leadership Team members for review and approval prior to publishing.

Any of the organization's operational or administrative staff can do the administrative work on creating, updating, and publishing these documents using the document management technology of choice.

CHANGE MANAGEMENT

This is the most common area that falls apart in day-to-day execution. Most companies do a good job of creating new programs, policies, procedures, etc. Yet they fail when it comes to managing changes to each of these. Why is change management so important? If you don't create and follow even a basic change management process, you will lose the quality and excellence in the Customer Life Cycle model execution and not benefit from maturing the effectiveness of the company and ensuring the results long term.

A change request can be a simple form published online within your intranet to which all team members have access. I would recommend that each organization create its own internal change management process with its internal leadership team. The forms can be customized by organization or topic area to simplify the process of submitting all requests to the appropriate Leadership Teams. If the change will impact other organizations or have a significant change to the customer's experience, then it may also require the approval of the Customer Experience Leadership team. Once the organization's leadership team approves the change, they can submit to the Customer Experience Team for review and approval if appropriate. The organization will then be responsible for executing the change using the best practice processes described in the methodology section of this book for rolling out changes. I recommend using one of the new online work management solutions for managing the changes as they allow for work flows, approvals, collaboration and documentation development and reviews as well. These solutions have made significant impact on enabling a more efficient capacity utilization of the team members including the operations team.

The following is an example of a change management form used to request a change to an element within the Customer Life Cycle model:

Figure 18. Sample change management form

Change Management Request Form
Change Request Number: <assigned by CLC Committee>

General Information		
Requestor Name		Date
Office/Dept		

Contact	Phone	Email	Text

Change Request Definition
Description – Describe the proposed change. (Please describe the CLC stage or process effected)
Justification – Justify why the proposed changes should be implemented.
Impact of Not Implementing – Explain the impact if the proposed change is not implemented.

Change Request Evaluation Analysis

Check each that apply

☐ Project Schedule	☐ Configuration Item	☐ Product Deliverables affected
☐ Project Costs	☐ Process Change	☐ Design Deliverables affected
☐ Project Scope	☐ Requirement Deliverables	☐ Metrics or Outcomes affected

Impact Description – Describe the impact for each of the items checked. List all deliverables affected by change request

Change Request Final Management Approval			
Final Approval Date	Name	Title	Recommendation
			☐ Approve ☐ Reject
Special Instructions – Provide any additional information regarding the final recommendation.			

In developing quality and excellence in the CX model delivery, one of the key success factors is a solid, well-executed communication plan. An effective communication plan supports the discussions of day-to-day activities, issues that arise, and the development and delivery of quick resolutions.

The diagram shows a top down and bottoms up communication plan, as illustrated in Figure 19:

Figure 19. Sample communication plan

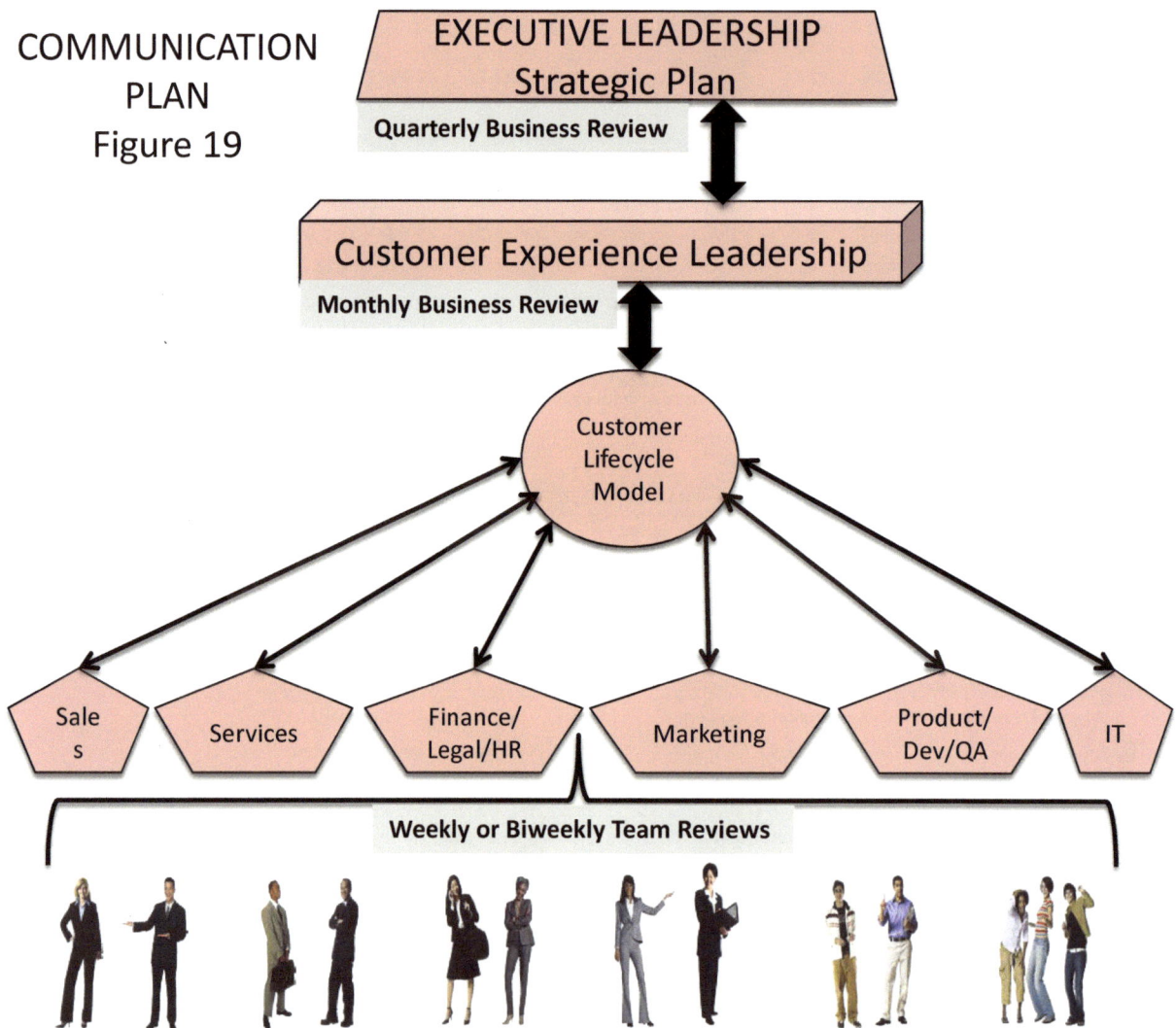

COMMUNICATION PLAN Figure 19

EXECUTIVE LEADERSHIP
Strategic Plan

Quarterly Business Review

Customer Experience Leadership

Monthly Business Review

Customer Lifecycle Model

Sales | Services | Finance/Legal/HR | Marketing | Product/Dev/QA | IT

Weekly or Biweekly Team Reviews

The layers of the communication plan ensure the customer information, decisions and messaging flows both upward and downward in an effective manner.

- Executive communication
- Leadership communication
- Team members' communication
- Communication rhythm

Executive communication: Key elements around the strategy.

It is vital for each organization's Executive to communicate a consistent message around the company's annual strategic plan, the annual top initiatives, goals, and objectives to the leadership team. The functional teams should discuss on a regular cadence the top concerns and issues about customer results, indicating what's working and what's not working. These discussions will arm the leadership team for each organization to represent their recommendations for making changes in the monthly and quarterly business reviews for how to improve the customer's success and value realized in a more consistent and standardized manner. The teams will feel empowered to be open with their thoughts and recommendations based on what they are seeing and earing from the customers they work with directly on a daily basis.

Leadership communication: The functional leadership team represents the middle management layer that represents the execution of the tactical plan and management of their teams. They usually are the leadership team that would communicate to each of their teams the Executive Strategic Plan and Department Strategic Plan that aligns to the Company Strategic Plan and Go to Market Plan. Their team meetings should communicate the same consistent message on the strategy, goals, and objectives both to their team members as well as sharing the Executives top concerns based on the results. They should discuss with the team how to modify or improve their current execution plan to help correct the areas that are not working well or that are not producing the planned results. It is also an opportunity to discuss if a strategy is worth pursuing and if some of their current plans should be modified or a new plan put in place that would drive to an improvement in the customer's experience and perception of value or return on their investment.

Team Member communication: The teams represent the various teams, groups or departments that would report up to the Functional leaders. These teams should voice their view of how things are really working at the ground floor, especially if they work directly with customers on a regular basis. The insight they can provide to the leadership team is valuable to understanding how the current strategy and tactical plans are working to create consistent results for the customers in each of the target markets. They see and hear from the customers and other internal team members what is causing some of the customer issues or concerns as well as the success stories. This critical information enables an understanding of the real areas that need to be addressed and what possible changes could be made to create a more loyal and entrenched customer. Often an entire plan or process doesn't need to be scrapped. Instead team members can create some modifications to the current plan that will shift just enough to provide the customer the value and experience that produces the desired results. Moreover, they can also tell you how the customers are responding to the new offerings, services, and product or process changes.

Team members are a great source of real information about how to provide better value and experiences to the customers based on the daily feedback they get from customer conversations. These team members will provide the best insight into how a customers perceive their experience with your products and services. Customer surveys will tell you part of the story, but the front line team members will tell you the rest of the story.

By providing an opportunity for team members to participate in the discussions of the strategic plan and what they think needs to be modified or added you can create a powerful buy-in that creates a sense of accountability and desire to see the changes succeed. Getting the teams behind the leaders is a powerful component to achieve success quickly with a focus on customer value and to sustain it over the long-term.

Communication Rhythm: *The schedule of various types of meetings or communication vehicles.*

There are several types of effective meetings. They are usually short, concise, and effective in making decisions quickly.

- Daily Stand ups
- Weekly Top Priorities
- Monthly Results Reviews
- Quarterly Business Strategy Reviews

This may seem like a lot of meetings. However, keep in mind, that the goal is to monitor the business actively in order to make decisions quickly, which, in turn, drive results more rapidly. If the team doesn't communicate regularly via a mechanism to engage in discussions, to receive answers, and to get approvals to act, then changes will happen too slowly and growth will lag rather than accelerate.

Here is a typical Communication Plan that would be setup for an organization.

Table 4. Sample communication plan

Meeting Type	When	People
Daily Stand Up	Mon – Fri at 10 a.m.	Team Members/Leader
Weekly Top Priorities	Mon 9 a.m.	Leadership Team/Executive
Weekly Top Priorities	Tues 9 a.m.	Team Leads/Leadership (Director/Manager)
Monthly Business Review	First Wed after Month close 2p.m.	Leadership Team/Executive
Monthly All Hands	Second Monday after Month Close 9 a.m. (replaces daily standups and weekly top priority meetings)	All Team Members/Leadership/Executive
Quarterly Business Strategy Review	Second Tues after quarter close 9 a.m.	Leadership Team/Executive

These communications sessions would be scheduled on everyone's calendar as established meetings in a regular rhythm. There will always be exceptions that you can adjust for as required. However, the best policy is to make these meetings mandatory unless a team member has their leader's approval not to attend. You may have to adjust times for worldwide situations to accommodate for various time zones. With the current global markets, many companies are worldwide and have a significant number of remote employees. The new technologies allow for inclusion of all employees to attend in a live video conference that can also be recorded for any employee that is unable to attend to review at a later time frame.

The agenda for each of these meetings can be customized to be the most effective to enable and equip the teams to be successful in their daily execution. The main topics are usually the following:

Daily Stand Ups

- Top Customer Issues
- Tactical areas of customer life cycle not working
- Concerns/Questions/Clarifications
- Customer Success Story

Weekly Top Priorities

- Top priority Customer Issues/Concerns
- Major product areas, processes or offerings not working
- Top Customer strategies that need to be addressed (High dollar)
- Change Management discussions and decisions

Monthly Results Reviews

- Review Customer Dashboard by Market Segment
- Review Customer Feedback trends (product, services, process, pricing, offerings, etc.)
- Review Company Results by Market Segment in a drill down structure to planned smart goals
- Review Organizational Dashboard
- Review Actuals to Budget and Forecast
- Customers at Risk and Plan of Action
- Hiring Plan
- Progress of top organizational Initiatives
- Change Management discussions

Quarterly Business Strategy Review

- Review Company Dashboard
- Review Actuals to Budget and Forecast
- New or changes for Budget Considerations
- Organization Headcount Plan
- Progress of top company Initiatives
- Is Strategy Working? Why or Why Not?
- Change Management discussions

The communication plan provides the team with a consistent opportunity to evolve and improve the execution details behind the Customer Life Cycle model and also to determine when and how to pivot on the strategy.

The Next Phase Plan

As discussed earlier, a Customer Life Cycle model is an iterative execution plan. Therefore, the Customer Experience Team will always be planning the next phase of evolution as the company grows.

Using the Gap Analysis from the Design stage, the CX team will evaluate the next set of priorities for implementation and put a project plan together with assignments and timeline for the next phase of the CX implementation. The CX team should review and approve the plan. This plan will become the key set of deliverables for the appropriate organizations to focus on for the next quarter.

The team will plan from quarter to quarter modifying the plan as required in order to continue delivering on the company goals and objectives following the strategic plan for evolving the Customer Life Cycle.

Evaluating the customer feedback each month may require a modification to your current plan based on the impact it could have on your ability to drive to results in a timely manner by creating consistent customer success. This means if you are not creating a Gold Customer (Loyal and Entrenched Customer) 10 out of 10 times consistently quarter in and quarter out, then you need to spend the time on the customer feedback content to determine what changes are required immediately to get to these results consistently.

As your organization matures in their CX model, the evolution of the teams will enable them to become more innovative in their abilities to find cost effective ways to better serve the customer and provide more value consistently.

The CX team should remain intact and meet on a frequency that allows the functional areas to continue to collaborate and innovate within each Customer Life Cycle section. This will keep the company focused on being Customer Centric and make this the new corporate way of life.

CHAPTER 10

KEY CONCEPTS TO TAKE AWAY

To build a successful working CX model requires an entire company dedicated to customer success as a way of life. Theories are great to understand what you want and need to accomplish as a company with a CX model. However, at some point you have to dig in and turn an attractive theory into an executable plan.

The company must buy into the CX model as a companywide commitment. It doesn't work to just create a customer success team in the hope that they can make all things happen for a customer to succeed and find real ROI. A customer's success takes a company commitment from the start of the first customer touch point with your company through every individual interaction they experience during their long term partnership with your company. To achieve this successful result, all organizations within the company should commit to a customer-centric corporate climate. They need to understand exactly how their contribution creates the right customer experience and perception from an engaging first impression all the way to becoming a long-term loyal customer who refers your company to all their colleagues due to the value you provide.

Once your company's leadership team invests in the idea of operating in a customer centric way of life, you will need a vision and a plan. The Customer Life Cycle creates the vision and the high level plan for the organizations to understand precisely how their role, responsibility, and accountability contributes to the delivery of the customer's success including what creates real value and a an impactful return on their investment.

You would then commit to creating a customer experience team, which will lead the development of journey maps for each section of the Customer Life Cycle. These journey maps will help create the detailed executable plan for each organization to begin executing this new way of life for the long-term. These plans will continue to evolve over time following the maturity model. The better your company becomes in executing, modifying and innovating their product, programs, standards, processes, procedures, and offerings the better their ability will be to deliver a consistent, quality, and engaged customer experience where your solution becomes indispensable.

The customer will become a true partner as they embed your solution into their business way of life, evolving along the maturity model roadmap with your solution at the heart of their innovation capability.

Look for podcasts and blogs on my website for on-going conversations on best practices in creating Customers for Life at www.landnexpand.com

ACKNOWLEDGMENTS

This book has been a work in progress for the last 20 years in the high tech industry. With each software company for whom I worked, I focused on the customer with a philosophy of *"Take care of the customer and the numbers will follow"*.

With this philosophy as my core methodology, I learned a tremendous amount by taking the time to understand each of my client's business strategy, operational models, corporate climate, the influential team members, and what their real problems were. I truly became a student that listened and learned from every customer. I must thank the hundreds of customers with whom I had the privilege of working over the years and who taught me so much about what was really important in building a long term partnership and real value.

I am grateful for the mentors throughout my career that believed in my passion to make a real impact on customers and their businesses and spent the time to nurture my abilities, knowledge and leadership skills to help me become a leader that made a difference.

Special thanks to Scott Maxwell, who encouraged me to turn my models and successful approach into workshops and an easy to follow program. He believed in the value I had to offer other companies and he inspired me to write a book that would be interesting and compelling for any growth company. His words of faith and support led me to spend the time to articulate this systematic approach into an easy to follow roadmap.

Finally, I thank Gerald Golden, my son, who helped me to design the illustrations and diagrams throughout the book and manage all of the marketing for the book and our company, LandNExpand, LLC. I thank, Darlene Staker, for the fabulous book cover design as well as their creativity and genius in marketing was crucial to the success of the book.

www.ingramcontent.com/pod-product-compliance
Lightning Source LLC
Chambersburg PA
CBHW041729210326
41598CB00008B/828